ROGER PROTZ

THE REAL ALE DRINKER'S ALMANAC

FOREWORD BY ANDREA GILLIES
EDITOR OF CAMRA'S GOOD BEER GUIDE

LOCHAR PUBLISHING · MOFFAT · SCOTLAND

Published by Lochar Publishing Ltd
No 7 & 8, The Holm
MOFFAT DG10 9JU
Tel: 0683 20916

British Library Cataloguing in Publication Data
Protz, Roger
  The Real Ale Drinker's Almanac
  1. Great Britain. Beers
  I. Title
  641.2'3

  ISBN 0-948403-18-7

Typeset in 9 on 10pt Times by
Hewer Text, Edinburgh
and printed in Great Britain by
The Eagle Press plc, Blantyre, Glasgow

CONTENTS

Acknowledgements	4
Foreword	5
Introduction	6
SCOTLAND	14
NORTH-EAST ENGLAND	31
YORKSHIRE	42
CENTRAL ENGLAND	76
EASTERN ENGLAND	121
THAMES VALLEY	149
LONDON	160
SOUTH-EAST ENGLAND	168
SOUTH-WEST ENGLAND	185
THE WEST COUNTRY	216
WALES	240
NORTH-WEST ENGLAND	252
NORTHERN IRELAND	276
ISLE OF MAN	278
GUERNSEY	281
Index	284

ACKNOWLEDGEMENTS

Thanks to Dr Keith Thomas of the Brewers Laboratory
(Brewlab), City of London Polytechnic, for "profiling my tongue"
and explaining in layman's language the mysteries of
fermentation, esters, and off flavours in beer. The timescale for
writing this book made it impossible for me to taste every available
cask beer produced in Britain and my friends and colleagues in the
British Guild of Beer Writers helped with views on some beers in
places that were difficult to reach; thanks in particular to Michael
Jackson, chairman of the guild and author of the seminal New
World Guide to Beer and Pocket Beer Book, Brian Glover, whose
New Beer Guide and CAMRA Dictionary of Beer have been
much thumbed in recent months, and Graham Lees. Thanks, too,
to Huw Rees in Cardiff and Tony Dean in Belfast. As always I
must pay my respects to the Campaign for Real Ale, both
collectively and severally. Many of the beers in this book would
not exist but for their astonishing voluntary endeavours over the
past 18 years. As a writer on beer I acknowledge my great debt to
the foot soldiers of the Campaign.

My grateful thanks to the brewers who put up with my letters
and incessant phone calls. Many have given—for the first time in
published form—considerable information about their recipes.
The information revealed will be of enormous interest to beer
lovers. To those brewers who have given little or no information
on the grounds of commercial secrecy it is worth pointing out that
rival brewers could determine their recipes by quite simple tests
and, more importantly, consumers have a right to know what goes
into the beers they pay for. If you draw the wrong conclusions
about the secret beers, the brewers have only themselves to blame.
The criterion for inclusion in the book has been "commercial
brewer", which means that I have included only those home-brew
pubs that sell their products to other outlets.

The word "independent" appears frequently. It should not
mask the fact that 80 per cent of British beer production is
controlled by the six major national companies, Bass, Allied
Breweries, Grand Metropolitan, Whitbread, Courage, and
Scottish and Newcastle.

Useful addresses

Brewlab, c/o Department of Biology, City of London Polytechnic,
Old Castle Street, London E1 7NT (01-283 1030 ext 413). Courses
for commercial brewers, home brewers and lay people, including a
beer tasting course sent through the post for people outside
London.
Campaign for Real Ale Ltd (CAMRA), 34 Alma Road, St
Albans, Herts AL1 3BW (0727 67201). Annual membership £9.

FOREWORD

Our mild and bitter ales, stouts and barley wines, in short, our beers, are a unique inheritance of Britain. Beer should be revered, understood and drunk in equal proportions in the same way as wine is today.

Sadly, in many quarters beer has a public image which is less than ideal. It is also extremely unfashionable, unless it is a bottled lager with a foreign name. To many people, beer is for swilling, beer is brown, beer is boring. It all tastes the same. Nothing could be further from the truth, as this excellent guide helps establish.

To make this quantum leap from general neglect to Great British Obsession, beer not only needs its own vocabulary, but people to use that vocabulary imaginatively. Roger Protz is not afraid to talk about citric acidity and explosions of fruit, nor is he afraid to be outspoken—his regional round-ups explain not only the brewing traditions of an area, but also how it regards its own beers. Fascinating information on ingredients has been volunteered by many breweries, and Roger's own tasting notes are an appetising introduction to the complexities of our regional beer styles.
Enjoy!

ANDREA GILLIES
Editor, CAMRA Good Beer Guide

INTRODUCTION

The British have rekindled a great interest in their idiosyncratic island beer style at a time when it is under intense attack from a mass marketed, poor imitation of the type of beer the rest of the world drinks. Lager may now account for almost half the beer sold in Britain but cask-conditioned beer— "real ale" as it is popularly known—is staging a remarkable resurgence.

The reasons are complex. There is a reaction against the moronic "lager loutism" associated with the Euro-drink. The end of the "baby boom" means that an older and wiser population looks for quality and tradition in beer as well as value for money. Almost twenty years of championing by the Campaign for Real Ale is now paying dividends through increased consumer awareness of the product and a fast growing membership of the movement. And there is the renowned British love of fair play and support for the underdog: if our beer is under attack then it is time we showed some concern for it.

Interest is heightened by knowledge. Other countries produce some of their beers by the method of warm or top fermentation, but most of it is found in bottled form. In Britain we drink the greater proportion of our beer on draught and real ale, uniquely, comes to fruition through a secondary fermentation in the cask rather as champagne reaches maturity in the bottle. It is that conditioning in the cask that gives the beer its ripeness of flavour and depth of character, and aromas and palates sharply different to those produced by cold or bottom fermentation.

Beer of great quality, produced by craftsmen, is as deserving of consideration as fine wine. Enormous attention is given to the product of the grape while the fruit of the barley tends to be tipped down indiscriminate throats. But it takes more skill

to make good beer than wine and the end result
demands greater respect. The variety of malt and
the blend of hops gives each beer its own character
and charm. As well as a good "beery" taste in the
mouth, there are a myriad bouquets and aromas
redolent of fields of grain and orchards of hops. This
book is a small contribution towards unlocking
those tastes and flavours.

The language of beer
People in the north of England speak of "mashing
the tea". Throughout Britain you will still hear the
expression "the tea is brewing". Tea is a latecomer
to these isles and the expressions have been handed
on from the days when all households, humble and
mighty, brewed their own ale as the staple beverage
and an important part of the family diet.

Brewing beer is not unlike making tea. Both are
the result of a simple infusion of basic ingredient
and hot water. The analogy can be extended: the
finished taste of the product depends crucially on
the variety of tea or malt used. A Lapsang
Souchong is smoky and intense, an Earl Gray light,
quenching and aromatic. Similarly an ale brewed
from pale malt will have a bouquet and palate
radically different to a beer made from darker malt
with a dash of roasted barley.

In the brewery the mash tun is the tea pot. The
malt that comes pouring into the vessel from a grain
hopper has been carefully nurtured by specialist
maltsters. Only a small proportion of the barley
grown in Britain is suitable for brewing. It must be
high in starch and low in nitrogen so that the sugars
can be easily extracted and it must sprout quickly.
In the maltings the grain is immersed in tanks of
water and encouraged to germinate by soaking up
the liquid. The wet grain is then spread on malting
floors in warm, dry rooms and within a few days
shoots break through the husk. The cells of the
barley are broken down by germination, making

the conversion to sugar possible.

When the maltster judges that partial germination has taken place satisfactorily, he moves the malt to a kiln where it is heated by hot air to stop further germination. The heat is gradually increased to produce the type of malt needed by the brewer: a pale, golden beer requires a lightly kilned malt; tawny ales will have a proportion of amber or crystal malt; dark beers, porters and stouts, will have chocolate or black malts that have been kilned to the point where there is little fermentable sugar content left but which are vital for both colour and flavour.

At the brewery the malt is crushed in a mill into a coarse powder known as grist. The brewer may use just one type of malt in the mash tun or he may blend pale and crystal with a dash of chocolate according to the recipe. Stouts and porters may have some unmalted roasted barley and, controversially, many brewers use adjuncts—wheat flour, torrefied wheat or barley, and maize—for cheapness, to counter protein haze and to encourage a lively head on the finished beer. The stronger the beer, the greater the amount of grist that is used. It is mixed in the mash tun with pure hot water (called liquor) either from the public supply or from the brewery's own wells. Many brewers add salts to the water to reproduce the hardness found in the water of Burton on Trent, which is considered ideal for brewing bitter beers.

The thick porridge lies in the tun for an hour or two. During this time the sugars are released from the malt and dissolve in the liquor. Temperature in the tun and the length of time the grist lies in the vessel have to be carefully judged in order to extract the maximum amount of sugar. When the brewer is satisfied, the sweet liquid—called wort—is run out of the bottom of the mash tun through a slotted base. The thick slurry of grain lies on the bottom of the tun and is then sprayed or sparged with more hot liquor to extract any remaining sugars. An individual brew is known as a "gyle"; by adjusting the amount of liquor, some brewers make more than one beer from a brew or, by adding different amounts of priming sugars and hops, will produce several beers of the same strength. This is known as "party gyling".

The wort is pumped to a copper where it is boiled vigorously with hops. The rise of Euro-lager in Britain has led to a fall in demand for English hop varieties but the brewers who have given some indication of their recipes for this book still have a great attachment to such traditional strains as Fuggles and Goldings from Kent and Worcestershire. The hop is a climbing plant with remarkable properties. Its blossom—the cone—contains tannins, resins and oils that not only add the classic bitterness to beer but also help to clarify the wort, kill bacteria and reduce protein haze. The hops used in a particular brew may be a blend of several strains. The brewer does not necessarily tip in all the hops at the start of the boil. The classic recipe often entails Fuggles, with their tangy bitterness, being added when the boil starts, with Goldings, renowned for their resiny aroma, added later. If the whole flower of the hop is used, they settle on the base of the copper and act as a filter when the boil is finished. If the hops have been compressed into pellets, the hopped wort will be filtered in a whirlpool centrifuge. While the wort is in the copper many brewers add sugar to encourage a strong fermentation and also as a cheap substitute for malt. The use of sugar in brewing was illegal until Mr Gladstone's Budget of 1880; many purists prefer not to use it today.

The hopped wort is cooled and then pumped to fermenting vessels in preparation for the violent confrontation with yeast. Before yeast is added the excise officer takes a dip with a hydrometer to measure the amount of sugars present in the wort.

Brewers have to pay duty on what is known as the wort's original or starting gravity; the higher the level of sugar, the more tax is levied and the stronger the finished beer.

Now the decks are cleared for the great battle between sweet wort and sugar-hungry yeast and it is this stage that marks the great divide between ale and lager. Ales—mild, bitter, stout, porter, old ales and barley wines—are fermented by a top fermenting yeast strain that works quickly and vigorously at a warm temperature (59-77°F/15-25°C). Breweries cultivate their own yeast strains and guard them with enormous care. Some, such as the Bass strain at Burton, can be more than a hundred years old. Each strain, along with the malt and the hops, imparts strong, individual flavours to beer; remove a yeast from one brewery and transfer it to another and within weeks it will have added new dimensions to the palate of the beer.

Yeast is pitched into the wort and vigorously mixed. Slowly a thin scum appears on the top of the wort. Bubbles burst to the surface, the scum becomes a foam and within twenty four hours it has transformed itself into a white-yellow-brown heaving crust. Above the fermenters, the air is heavy and heady with the aromas of raw alcohol and carbon dioxide. The head of yeast is skimmed off and the remainder slowly sinks to the bottom of the vessel as the sugars are converted. Brewers control the amount of sugar left in the beer. No beer has all the sugars fermented out, for the finished brew would be uncomfortably dry. Higher gravity beers tend to be sweeter than lower gravity ones. The amount of sugar left is known as the degree of attenuation.

Warm fermentation takes about a week. The raw or green beer is run into conditioning tanks and left to mature for a few days. Conditioning allows the beer to purge itself of the rough, unpleasant flavours produced by fermentation. Finings or isinglass, a glutinous substance made from the swim bladder of the sturgeon, is added to force the remaining yeast in the beer to settle, and priming sugar is also inserted to encourage a strong secondary fermentation. Brown roasted sugar—caramel—is sometimes added to give colour; as caramel is an E number many brewers prefer not to use it. After a few days in the tanks the beer is racked into casks, either metal or wood, and bunged. Extra priming sugar is sometimes added at this stage and some brewers put in a handful of hops to give a good floral or resiny aroma.

The beer that now leaves the brewery is not yet ready to be drunk. It is in the pub cellar that it undergoes its secondary fermentation in the cask. As the remaining yeast settles to the belly of the cask it continues to transform the last of the sugar into alcohol. The skill of the cellarman, using porous venting pegs placed in the bunghole on top of the cask to control the escape of natural gas, determines when conditioning is complete and the mature beer, redolent with good malt, hop and fruit aromas, is ready to be served.

The taste of beer
The nose or bouquet of a beer and its flavour in the mouth are predominantly malty and hoppy. But there are other aromas and tastes produced by fermentation. As yeast turns sweet sugars into alcohol and carbon dioxide it produces what are known as esters. In a low gravity beer, where the predominate aroma will be that of the hops, esters may be present in the form of a slight citric fruitiness. In stronger beers with a higher malt content fruitiness is apparent in a riper fashion and banana, apple, pear drops and gooseberry are common. Crystal and amber malts give a pleasing nut character while dark and black malts add a touch of chocolate, coffee, burnt toast and

liquorice. In barley wines there is often a powerful
winey aroma with strong hints of tannin, leather,
dried or glaće fruit and pineapple.

This guide encourages drinkers to use their noses
as well as their tastebuds. The nose or bouquet of a
top-fermented beer is often slow to develop. Beer
should be kept at a cellar temperature of 55°F/12°C;
the aromas begin to come out as the beer warms up
in the glass. Drink some beer to leave room to give
the glass a good swirl to help release the nose and
then give a deep sniff. As the temperature of the
beer rises the predominate grain and hop characters
will be joined by other aromas produced by
fermentation. Agitate the beer in the mouth to get
the full flavour of the liquid and let it slowly trickle
over the tongue; the tongue recognises sweetness at
the front, saltiness and sourness in the middle and
bitterness at the back. "Finish" refers to the
after-taste of the beer. The dryness of a beer is often
wrongly associated with hops. In fact dryness and
even astringency come from the malt.

Beer tasting is a highly subjective assessment and
the aroma and palate of a beer can change from one
brew to another and from one year's crop of barley
and hops—though careful blending of ingredients
will remove any sharp differences. My views are not
the last word and response from other drinkers and
brewers is welcome. One word of advice: it is
always best to drink beer close to its brewery of
origin. Delivery, storage and poor cellar work can
result in famous beers being almost unrecognisable.
Draught Bass and Boddingtons Bitter are classic
examples of superb beers that often taste either thin
or cloying in the notoriously unreliable London free
trade. The method of dispense is also vital to the
palate of beer. While beers of central and southern
England are served with a small head of foam,
Yorkshire beers lose their tart hop character if they
are not served through a sparkler that produces a
dense collar of foam. Scottish beers best produce

their characteristic rounded dark maltiness when
served by the traditional method of air pressure and
a tall fount.

The strength of beer
Two systems are used in this guide to indicate the
strength of beer. Original gravity is not strictly a
guide to strength but is a measure for tax purposes
of the fermentable sugars present in the wort.
Water has a gravity or density of 1000°. A beer with
an OG of 1036° will have 36 parts of sugar present in
the water. It is a useful but not full-proof indication
of the finished strength of a beer; a 1036° beer is
weaker than a 1050° one. Brewers are now
introducing the system of Alcohol By Volume,
which is a measure of the alcohol present in a
finished beer. The OG and the ABV are often
identical, ie 1036° OG and 3.6% ABV. I have not,
however, attempted to guess the ABVs where
brewers have not reported them as there can be a
substantial difference between OG and ABV
depending on the degree of attenuation of a brew.

Further reading
CAMRA's annual Good Beer Guide should be an
inseparable companion for all lovers of fine ale. It
lists some 5000 pubs throughout the British Isles
that serve cask beer as well as specialist off-licences.
Its brewery section lists all cask and bottle
conditioned beers. 1990 edition: £6.95. Michael
Jackson's New World Guide to Beer (£15.95) is a
superb illustrated guide to the great ales and lagers
of the world. Brian Glover's New Beer Guide
(£3.95) lists all the small micro-brewers in Britain
and his Dictionary of Beer (£2.95) is a valuable
pocket book of information. The Great British
Book (£5.95) by myself is a history of British
brewing from pre-Roman to modern times. All
these books are available from CAMRA, 34 Alma
Road, St Albans, Herts AL1 3BW. Add £1 post and
packing per volume.

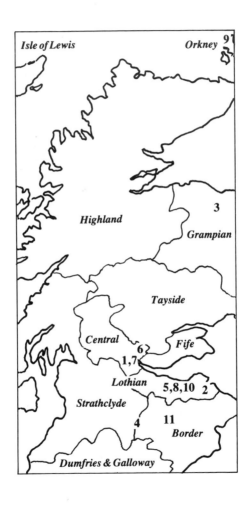

SCOTLAND

With the exception of the tiny Borve and Orkney breweries, Scotland's brewing industry is based in the Lowlands. The concentration of breweries around Alloa, Edinburgh and Glasgow was encouraged by the fact that the best barley for malting grew in the Borders and North East England. Further north, barley that survives the hard climate is best suited for distilling. Traditional Scottish beer is quite different in character to English ale. Roasted barley or dark and chocolate malt give a darker and nut-sweet character to beer and the lack of a hop industry means that hops are used more sparingly. Beer terms are different, too: low gravity ale is called "light", even when it is dark or walnut brown in colour, medium ale is "heavy" while stronger "Export" ale recalls the great, pioneering days of Scottish brewing when the likes of Younger refreshed the American, Indian and Australian colonies. The terms 60/-, 70/-, 80/- and 90/- refer to a 19th century system of invoicing beers according to strength. While handpumps and beer engines are now widespread, the traditional method of serving Scottish beer is the tall fount primed by air pressure.

1   Alloa Brewery Company Ltd

Whins Road, Alloa, Clackmannanshire, Central FK10 3RB Tel: 0259 723539

Subsidiary of Allied Breweries
Reception centre No. *Brewery tours* Yes

ARCHIBALD ARROL'S 70/-
OG 1037° ABV 3.5%
Ingredients not revealed

TASTING NOTES

Nose	Pleasing hop resin aroma, hints of orange and lemon fruit
Palate	Light maltiness with delicate hop finish
Comments	Good session beer, well hopped for a Scottish ale

ARCHIBALD ARROL'S 80/-
OG 1042° ABV 4.2%
Ingredients not revealed

TASTING NOTES

Nose	Rich fruit nose with hint of butterscotch and hop resin
Palate	Sweet maltiness in the mouth, dry, slightly astringent finish
Comments	Ripe and fruity heavy beer

2 Belhaven Brewery Company Ltd

**Dunbar, East Lothian EH42 1RS
Tel: 0368 62734**

Independent, owned by Control Securities
Reception centre Yes. *Brewery tours* by arrangement

BELHAVEN 60/-

OG 1030.5° ABV 3%
Ingredients: Golden Promise
pale malt (89%), black malt
(4%) liquid sugar (7%).
Fuggles, Goldings and British
Columbian Bramlings hops

TASTING NOTES

Nose	Light hop and grain aroma
Palate	Pronounced maltiness with delicate dry finish
Comments	Delicious drinkable mild with lovely walnut brown colour

BELHAVEN 70/-

OG 1035.5° ABV 3.5%
Ingredients: Golden Promise pale malt (89%), black
malt (1%), crystal malt (1.5%), liquid sugar (7%).
Fuggles, Goldings and British Columbian Bramlings
hops.

TASTING NOTES

Nose	Hop flower and glacé fruit aroma
Palate	Nutty on the tongue with light, sweet finish
Comments	Delectable honey-coloured session beer

BELHAVEN 80/-

OG 1041.5° ABV 4.1%
Ingredients: Golden Promise pale malt (86%), black
malt (1.5%), crystal malt (2.5%), liquid sugar (10%).
Fuggles, Goldings and British Columbian Bramlings
hops

TASTING NOTES

Nose	Stunning aroma of rich grain, gooseberry, hop flower and toast
Palate	Mouth-filling balance of malt and tart fruit with intense dry finish
Comments	Memorable rounded ale, a complex mix of fruit and hop. Wonderful companion for strong cheese and shell fish.

BELHAVEN 90/-

OG 1070° ABV 7.5%
Ingredients: Golden Promise pale malt (84%), black
malt (4%), liquid sugar (12%). Fuggles, Goldings and
British Columbian Bramlings hops.

TASTING NOTES

Nose	Light hop aroma, hints of pineapple
Palate	Rich maltiness with powerful hop finish and dark chocolate notes
Comments	A rich, warming old ale that keeps out the chill. A beer to be sipped and savoured

3   Borve Brew House

Ruthven by Huntly, Aberdeenshire, Grampian AB5 4SR Tel: 046687 343

Independent
Reception centre in public house attached. *Brewery tours* Yes

BORVE ALE

OG 1040° ABV 3.7%
Ingredients: pale malt
(97%) crystal malt (1½%),
chocolate malt (½%), roast
barley (1%). Whole and
pellet Goldings hops.

TASTING NOTES

Nose	Delicate hop aroma with roast grain notes
Palate	Rich rounded malt taste with long bitter finish and hint of chocolate
Comments	A fine reddish-brown Scots ale with deep malt and hop character

BORVE EXTRA STRONG ALE

OG 1085° ABV 10%
Ingredients: pale malt (92%), crystal malt (8%).
Whole and pellet Goldings hops.

TASTING NOTES

Nose	Rich fruit and grain promise from ruby red ale
Palate	Intense mouth-filling smokiness with deep hop finish
Comments	Polished professional strong beer brewed by father and son in converted schoolhouse

4   Broughton Brewery Ltd

Broughton, by Biggar, Lanarkshire, Strathclyde ML12 6HQ Tel: 08994 345

Independent
Reception centre No. *Brewery tours* by arrangement

GREENMANTLE ALE

OG 1038° ABV 4%
Ingredients: pale malt,
"negligible" % of
roasted barley.
Fuggles and Goldings
pellet hops.

TASTING NOTES

Nose	Copper-coloured beer with pronounced orange- and-lemon-slices aroma
Palate	Rich maltiness with deep fruit finish
Comments	A no-nonsense brew with a powerful bitter-sweet appeal. Broughton Special Bitter is the same brew as Greenmantle Ale but dry hopped for English market; more hop character on the nose

MERLIN'S ALE

OG 1044°
Ingredients: pale malt, small % of roasted barley.
Fuggles and Goldings pellet hops

TASTING NOTES

Nose	Delicate aromas of hop and grain with fruit notes developing
Palate	Rounded, mouth-filling malt and hop with deep finish and fruit notes
Comments	Luscious golden brew

Old Jock (OG 1070°) is a dark and fruity bottled beer with roast barley notes occasionally sold in draught form.

5 Caledonian Brewery Company Ltd

Slateford Road, Edinburgh, Lothian EH11 1PH
Tel: 031-337 1286

Independent
Reception centre No. *Brewery tours* Yes

CALEDONIAN 70/-
OG 1036° ABV 3.3%
Ingredients: Golden Promise malt, crystal malt, amber malt, chocolate malt, black malt, wheat malt. Fuggles and Goldings whole hops

TASTING NOTES

Nose	Light hints of Ovaltine and hop resin
Palate	Good mouth balance of malt and hop with bitter-sweet finish
Comments	Fine refreshing amber session brew

CALEDONIAN PORTER
OG 1042° ABV 4%
Ingredients: Golden Promise malt, crystal malt, amber malt, chocolate malt, black malt, wheat malt. Fuggles and Goldings whole hops

TASTING NOTES

Nose	Rich aromas of roasted barley and black chocolate
Palate	Biscuity in the mouth, dry finish with good hop character
Comments	Dark and delectable brew

CALEDONIAN 80/-
OG 1043° ABV 4.1%
Ingredients: Golden Promise malt, crystal malt, amber malt, chocolate malt, wheat malt. Fuggles and Goldings whole hops

TASTING NOTES

Nose	Rich promise of grain and hops, developing citric notes
Palate	Fat grain in mouth, deep dry hop finish with chocolate notes
Comments	Superbly balanced golden heavy

MERMAN XXX

OG 1052° ABV 4.9%
Ingredients: Golden Promise malt, crystal malt, amber malt, chocolate malt, black malt, wheat malt. Fuggles whole hops

TASTING NOTES

Nose	Deep bouquet of hop resins, chocolate and ripe fruit
Palate	Complex balance of malt, biscuit, fruit and hop bitterness, long dry finish with chocolate notes
Comments	Warming, rounded dark beer, called Merman because it makes you "legless".

CALEDONIAN STRONG ALE

OG 1078° ABV 7.6%
Ingredients: Golden Promise malt, crystal malt, amber malt, chocolate malt, black malt, wheat malt. Fuggles and Goldings whole hops

TASTING NOTES

Nose	Assault of hop resin, malt, fruit and nut with apple hints
Palate	Mouth filling grain and hop, intense, dry vinous finish
Comments	Superb old ale, excellent with Stilton. Fermented for 10-12 days to remove any sweet cloying on palate. Sold in US as MacAndrew's Strong Ale

6   Harviestoun Brewery Ltd

**Dollar, Clackmannanshire, Central FK14 7LX
Tel: 02594 2141**

Independent
Reception centre Yes. *Brewery tours* by arrangement

HARVIESTOUN 80/-
OG 1040
Ingredients: pale malt (92%),
crystal malt (8%) with soft
brown sugar added in copper.
Fuggles and Goldings hop
pellets; dry hopped with Styrian
Goldings whole hops.

TASTING NOTES

Nose	Pleasing hop field aroma
Palate	Maltiness balanced by quenching hop flavour and long dry finish
Comments	A refreshing beer with great hop character for Scottish brew

OLD MANOR
OG 1050°
Ingredients: pale malt (93%), crystal malt (6%),
chocolate malt (1%) with soft brown sugar added in
copper. Goldings and Northern Brewer hop pellets;
dry hopped with Styrian Goldings whole hops.

TASTING NOTES

Nose	Powerful hop aroma with rich fruit developing
Palate	Mouth filling balance of malty sweetness and hop bitterness; nutty roast and chocolate notes in the long dry finish
Comments	Rounded beer of great character, a fine end-of-session strong ale.

7   Maclay & Company Ltd

**Thistle Brewery, Alloa, Central FK10 1ED
Tel: 0259 723387**

Independent
Reception centre Yes. *Brewery tours* Trade only

60/- PALE ALE
OG 1034° ABV 3.2%
Ingredients: 100% Scottish
Golden Promise barley with
caramel for colour. Whole
Fuggles hops.

TASTING NOTES

Nose	Light hop and biscuity aroma
Palate	Rich grain and hop with vanilla tones in light dry finish
Comments	Potable dark ale with chewy malt appeal; excellent session beer

70/- SPECIAL
OG 1034° ABV 3.2%
Ingredients: 100% Scottish Golden Promise barley
with caramel for colour. Whole Fuggles hops

TASTING NOTES

Nose	Delicate, pleasing hop aroma
Palate	Refreshing balance of grain and bitterness with lingering dry finish
Comments	Delicious quenching copper-coloured ale

80/- EXPORT
OG 1039° ABV 4.2%
Ingredients: 100% Scottish Golden Promise barley
with caramel for colour. Whole Fuggles hops.

TASTING NOTES

Nose	Strong hop bouquet with rich fruit developing
Palate	Full, rounded maltiness offset by hop bitterness; long finish with creamy vanilla notes underlying the dryness
Comments	A fine example of a rich Scottish Export, a good companion for strong-flavoured food

PORTER

OG 1040° ABV 4.1%
Ingredients: 100% Scottish Golden Promise barley with caramel for colour. Whole Fuggles hops

TASTING NOTES

Nose	Light hop and grain aroma
Palate	Fat, chewy malt in mouth, with dry hop and toast finish
Comments	Tasty, delectable dark ale

8 McEwan and Younger

Fountain Brewery, Fountain Bridge, Edinburgh, Lothian EH3 9YY Tel: 031-229 9377

Trading name of Scottish and Newcastle Breweries
Reception centre Yes. *Brewery tours* Yes
*With the exception of Younger No 3, McEwan and Younger cask beers are identical brews

McEWAN 70/-; YOUNGER SCOTCH

in Scotland and NE England;

YOUNGER BITTER

in other parts of England

OG 1036.5° ABV 3.7%
Ingredients: Scotch ale
malt, roast barley,
maize, wheat and cane
sugar. English and
Hallertau whole and
pellet hops

TASTING NOTES

Nose	Light grain notes with delicate fruit developing
Palate	Creamy on the tongue with short, dry finish and vanilla notes
Comments	What brewers call "a background beer", lacking strong mouth appeal

McEWAN 80/-; YOUNGER IPA

OG 1043° ABV 4.5%
Ingredients: Scotch ale malt, roast barley, maize, wheat and cane sugar. English and Hallertau whole and pellet hops

TASTING NOTES

Nose	Strong grain character with citric fruit note
Palate	Mouth-filling maltiness with dry, slightly fruity finish
Comments	A pleasant, sweetish amber beer

YOUNGER NO 3

OG 1043° ABV 4.5%
Ingredients: Scotch ale malt, roast barley, maize, wheat and cane sugar. English and Hallertau whole and pellet hops

TASTING NOTES

Nose	Rich hop and biscuit aroma
Palate	Complex mix of chewy maltiness and bitter hop character. Intense dry finish with chocolate and nut notes
Comment	A distinctive malty dark Scottish ale

9   Orkney Brewery

Quoyloo, Sandwick, Orkney KW16 3LT
Tel: 0856 84 802

Independent
Reception centre No *Brewery tours* Yes

RAVEN ALE

OG 1038° ABV 4%
Ingredients: pale Scottish
malt (93%), wheat flour (7%)
plus roasted barley for
colour. Worcester Goldings
Variety and Fuggles hops

TASTING NOTES

Nose	Intense grain aroma with hints of plum jam
Palate	Stunning balance of grain, hop and fruit with complex finish of hoppy dryness and roast barley nuttiness
Comments	Delectable rounded ale with a fruitiness that suggests a higher gravity. Sold in filtered and pasteurised keg form on Orkney but finding increasing number of cask outlets in Scotland

10 Tennent Caledonian Breweries Ltd

Heriot Brewery, 15 Russell Road, Roseburn, Edinburgh, Lothian EH12 5NA Tel: 031-337 1361

Subsidiary of Bass
Reception centre No *Brewery tours* No

TENNENT'S 80/-

OG 1042° ABV 4.2%
Ingredients: not revealed "though
high % of Scottish pale malt from
Bass maltings at Alloa and no
artificial colourings or flavourings
are used". Whole English hops,
varieties not revealed.

TASTING NOTES

Nose	Light hop and grain aroma
Palate	Delicate malt and hop in the mouth, light hop finish
Comments	A pleasant, typical Bass ale; quite unlike a "heavy" beer

11   Traquair House Brewery

**Traquair House, Innerleithen, Peeblesshire,
Borders EH44 6PW Tel: 0896 830 323**

Independent
Reception centre No but beers can be drunk in tea
rooms. *Brewery tours* by arrangement

BEAR ALE

OG 1050° ABV 5%
Ingredients: 100% barley malt with small % of roasted
barley for colour. East Kent Goldings hops

TASTING NOTES

Nose	Rich grain and hop aroma with powerful marmalade fruit developing
Palate	Warm fruit and nut on palate, bitter-sweet finish with roast notes
Comments	Superb rounded traditional Scots heavy for drinking alone or as good companion for smoked fish, cheese or pasta dishes

TRAQUAIR HOUSE ALE

OG 1075° ABV 7%
Ingredients: 100% barley
for colour. East Kent Goldings

TASTING NOTES

Nose	Stunning aromas of grain, hop, dark chocolate, rich fruit and spices
Palate	Powerful vinous attack of grain and hop with intense bitter finish and strong hints of pineapple and chocolate
Comments	Dark, heady and potent brew—try it in place of port or madeira—produced by the Laird of Traquair in restored medieval brewhouse in grounds of stately house

NORTH-EAST ENGLAND

The North-east is a beery buffer between Scotland and the rest of England. When a Geordie calls for a "Scotch" he or she wants a beer, not a whisky, and they mean a brew, either produced locally or in Scotland, that is malty and lightly hopped. Vaux of Sunderland brew a specific beer to meet this demand—Lorimer's Best Scotch, based on the ale once brewed by Lorimer and Clark in Edinburgh. At the height of its popularity, the bulk of Lorimer's production was drunk not in Edinburgh but in the North-east via the Caledonian railway. Further south in Teesside drinkers demand powerful ales. Cameron's Strongarm, with a gravity of 1040 degrees, is considered a "session" beer, so much so that Camerons have introduced a stronger beer, Strongarm Premium, in order to have a full portfolio of ales. Camerons beers are brewed in two-floored "dropping" fermenters similar to Yorkshire stone squares (q.v), which give the finished products a high level of natural carbonation.

1   Big Lamp Brewery

1 Summerhill Street, Newcastle upon Tyne, Tyne & Wear NE4 6EJ Tel: 091-261 4227

Independent
Reception centre No. *Brewery tours* by arrangement

BIG LAMP BITTER

OG 1040°
Ingredients: 100% pale malt and crystal malt, 20% invert sugar in copper. Fuggles and English and Styrian Goldings whole hops

TASTING NOTES

Nose	Light, delicate aromas of grain and hop resin
Palate	Rounded balance of malt and hop with deep dry finish and orange peel notes
Comments	Superb, beautifully balanced copper-coloured ale with plenty of hop and fruit character; antidote to mass produced keg Geordie beers

PRINCE BISHOP ALE

OG 1044°
Ingredients: 100% pale malt, 16% invert sugar in copper. English and Styrian Goldings

TASTING NOTES

Nose	Rich aromas of grain, Goldings and fruit
Palate	Hearty mouth-filling malt with intense, complex finish of powerful hop and tart fruit
Comments	Deceptively strong, tangy pale bitter

SPECIAL

OG 1050°
Ingredients: pale malt (88%), crystal (12%), 15%
invert sugar in copper. English and Styrian Goldings
whole hops

TASTING NOTES

Nose	Fat malt aromas with hop and fruit notes
Palate	Vast plummy fruit and malt with deep, lingering finish full of great hop and fruit character
Comments	Stunning, complex dark copper ale

OLD GENIE

OG 1070°
Ingredients: pale malt (90%), crystal malt (10%), 11%
invert sugar in copper. Fuggles and English Goldings
whole hops

TASTING NOTES

Nose	Enormous bouquet of malt, Goldings and rich fruit
Palate	Heavy mouth-filling grain, vast bitter-sweet finish with complex banana and gooseberry notes
Comments	Sumptuous strong, complex dark beer. Big Lamp also brew Blackout (1100°) for beer festivals only; not tasted.

2   J W Cameron & Co Ltd

PO Box 21, Lion Brewery, Hartlepool, Cleveland TS24 7QS Tel: 0429 2666666

Independent owned by Brent-Walker PLC
Reception centre Yes. *Brewery tours* Yes

TRADITIONAL BITTER
OG 1036°
Ingredients: pale malt, crystal malt, flaked maize and brewing sugar. English Fuggles and Goldings hop pellets

TASTING NOTES

Nose	Delicate hop and grain aroma
Palate	Light balance of malt and hop with long dry finish and fruit notes
Comments	A tangy quaffing beer

STRONGARM
OG 1040°
Ingredients: pale malt, crystal malt, flaked maize and brewing sugar. English Fuggles and Goldings hop pellets

TASTING NOTES

Nose	Rich hop and grain with developing hints of orange peel
Palate	Round malt and fruit with long dry finish and vanilla hints
Comments	A beautifully crafted and complex ale

STRONGARM PREMIUM
OG 1045° ABV 4.1%
Ingredients: pale malt, crystal malt, flaked maize,
brewing sugar. English Fuggles and Goldings hop
pellets

TASTING NOTES

Nose	Rich promise of hop with citric notes
Palate	Powerful mouth-filling malt and fruit with bitter-sweet finish
Comments	Fine walnut-brown ale, a good companion for rich-flavoured food

3　Castle Eden

**PO Box 13 Castle Eden, Hartlepool, Cleveland
Tel: 0429 836431**

Subsidiary of Whitbread
Reception centre No. *Brewery tours* by arrangement

CASTLE EDEN ALE
OG 1040° ABV 4.2%
Ingredients: "white" (pale) malt (70%), torrefied
wheat (10%), sugar (20%). Hop extract (90%), Target
hop pellets (10%)

TASTING NOTES

Nose	Strong hop and blackcurrant jam aroma
Palate	Rich malt and fruit with delicate dry, hoppy finish
Comments	A refreshing medium-strength ale, good on its own or with food—an excellent ploughman's lunch beer

4   Northern Clubs Federation Brewery Ltd

**Lancaster Road, Dunston, Tyne & Wear NE11 9HR
Tel: 091 460 9023**

Independent clubs co-operative
Reception centre No. *Brewery tours* by arrangement

BEST BITTER
OG 1036° ABV 3.6%
Ingredients: English pale ale malt (75%), flaked maize
(10%), sugar (15%). Bramling Cross, Target and
Challenger hops

TASTING NOTES

Nose	Delicate fresh hop and grain
Palate	Good malt flavour on tongue, light bitter finish
Comments	A pleasant refreshing easy-drinking session beer

SPECIAL ALE
OG 1041° ABV 4%
Ingredients: English pale
ale malt (75%), flaked
maize (10%), sugar (15%).
Bramling Cross, Target and
Challenger hops

TASTING NOTES

Nose	Rich malt and fruit aroma
Palate	Warm rounded malt character with delicate hop finish
Comments	Well-crafted, polished beer

5 Hadrian Brewery Ltd

Unit 7, Foundry Lane Industrial Estate, Byker, Newcastle upon Tyne, Tyne & Wear NE6 1LH Tel: 091 276 5302

Independent
Reception centre No. *Brewery tours* by arrangement

GLADIATOR BITTER

OG 1030° ABV 4%
Ingredients: pale malt (99%), coloured malt (1%).
Goldings and Fuggles whole hops.

TASTING NOTES

Nose	Delicate fresh hop character
Palate	Mellow balance of hop and grain with light dry finish
Comments	A copper-coloured bitter with a good quenching taste

CENTURION BEST BITTER

OG 1045° ABV 4.6%
Ingredients: pale malt (99.5%), coloured malt (½%).
Goldings and Fuggles whole hops

TASTING NOTES

Nose	Rich promise of fruit and hop
Palate	Mouth-filling complex balance of malt and fruit, long dry, hoppy finish
Comments	Light-coloured characterful strong bitter

EMPEROR ALE

OG 1050° ABV 5.2%
Ingredients: pale malt (98%), coloured malt (2%).
Goldings hops.

TASTING NOTES

Nose	Light hop aroma, hints of liquorice
Palate	Rounded, warming fruit and grain in mouth with long dry finish and vanilla notes
Comments	A fine fireside old ale, with deep red colour

6 Newcastle Breweries Ltd

Tyne Brewery, Gallowgate, Newcastle upon Tyne, Tyne & Wear NE99 1RA Tel: 091 232 5091

Subsidiary of Scottish and Newcastle Breweries
Reception centre Yes. *Brewery tours* Yes.

THEAKSTON
BEST BITTER

OG 1037°
Ingredients: not revealed

TASTING NOTES

Nose	Delicate aroma of grain and hop
Palate	Light quenching balance of malt and grain with dry finish
Comments	Newcastle version of the beer is variable in quality; occasional "farmyard" aroma indicates sulphiting to prolong shelf life. Following closure of Theakston's Carlisle plant Best Bitter is now also being brewed at Masham, Yorkshire (q.v.).

7   Vaux Breweries Ltd

**The Brewery, Sunderland, Tyne & Wear SR1 3AN
Tel: 091 567 6277**

Independent
Reception centre Yes. *Brewery tours* Yes

LORIMER'S BEST SCOTCH

OG 1036° ABV 3.65%
Ingredients: Triumph malt (85%), glucose/invert
sugar (12%), roasted barley (3%). Fuggles and
Challenger hop pellets

TASTING NOTES

Nose	Light hop aroma with toast and caramel notes
Palate	Fat grain in mouth, dry finish with roasted coffee notes
Comments	A dark, good-drinking flavoursome beer

VAUX BEST BITTER

OG 1038° ABV 3.85%
Ingredients: Triumph malt (100%). Fuggles,
Challenger and Target hop pellets

TASTING NOTES

Nose	Delicate whiff of hop resin
Palate	Pleasing balance of grain and hop with dry finish
Comments	An easy drinking pale coloured bitter

SAMSON ALE

OG 1042° ABV 4.15%
Ingredients: Triumph malt (85%), glucose/invert
sugar (15%), caramel for colour. Fuggles, Challenger
and Target hop pellets

TASTING NOTES

Nose	Rich attack of hop and fat grain
Palate	Fine mouth-filling balance of grain and hop with long dry finish and banana and raisin hints
Comments	Fine sipping coppery ale, good for drinking on its own or with flavoursome food; Vaux Double Maxim (OG 1044° in bottle) is being test marketed in draught form

YORKSHIRE

Yorkshire's proud, prickly and insular attitudes are personified by the belief that the region's beers are the best in Britain. Certainly the appellation "Yorkshire bitter" has acquired something of a cult status in recent years although not all of those nationally-available brews are necessarily worthy of the name. The counties can lay claim to a singular style of ale brewing, based on the "Yorkshire stone square" system which originally used fermenting vessels made of local stone or slate. Today only Sam Smith of Tadcaster and Joshua Tetley of Leeds brew in squares. A Yorkshire square is made of two chambers. The lower section is filled with cooled hopped wort. When fermentation begins the yeast rises into the top chamber through a hole. The wort is then pumped into the top chamber and vigorously mixed with the yeast. When fermentation is complete the beer runs back into the bottom chamber. The high level of natural carbon dioxide produced during fermentation helps create the thick collar of foam on a pint which Yorkshire drinkers expect. There are still good tasty dark milds available in the region while bitters range from the delicate hop aroma of Theakston's through the quenching citric acidity of Tetley's to the explosion of fruit in Taylor's.

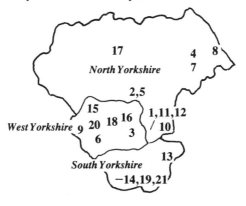

1   Bass (Tadcaster)

**Tower Brewery, Wetherby Road, Tadcaster
N Yorks LS24 9SD Tel: 0937 832361**

Subsidiary of Bass
*No information received

MILD XXXX
OG 1031°

TASTING NOTES

Nose	Light grain aroma
Palate	Malt in the mouth, short dry finish with some chocolate notes
Comments	Pleasant, easy-drinking dark mild ale

LIGHT 5 STAR
OG 1031°

TASTING NOTES

Nose	Delicate grain and hop bouquet
Palate	Malt in the mouth with slight hop edge, short bitter-sweet finish
Comments	Light session bitter

SPECIAL BITTER
OG 1036°

TASTING NOTES

Nose	Good grain aroma with slight fruit notes
Palate	Pronounced malt feel in the mouth with light hop, dry bitter-sweet finish
Comments	Easy drinking, typical Bass bitter

2   Big End Brewery

62A Otley Road, Harrogate, N Yorks HG2 0DP
Tel: 0423 503299

Independent micro-brewery set up in 1988; two pub outlets
Reception centre No. *Brewery tours* No

PISTON BITTER
OG 1038°
Ingredients not revealed

TASTING NOTES

Nose	Aromatic promise of hops
Palate	Quenching balance of grain and hop with light, delicate finish
Comments	Pleasant light session ale

OLD LUBRICATION
OG 1042°
Ingredients not revealed

TASTING NOTES

Nose	Rich hop and toast aroma
Palate	Fruit on the tongue, deep bitter finish with chocolate hints
Comments	Dark, malty ale

3 Clark

**Westgate Brewery, Wakefield, W. Yorks WF2 9SW
Tel: 0924 377527**

Independent
Reception centre Yes. *Brewery tours* Yes

CLARK'S HB
OG 1033°
Ingredients: pale malt, crystal malt (4%), chocolate
malt (1%), priming sugar. Challenger hops

TASTING NOTES

Nose	Delicate aroma of malt and hop
Palate	Light malt flavour, bitter-sweet finish
Comments	Easy-drinking session bitter

GARTHWAITE SPECIAL
OG 1035°
Ingredients: pale malt, crystal malt (4%), chocolate
malt (1%), priming sugar. Challenger hops

TASTING NOTES

Nose	Tart and tangy hop and grain aroma
Palate	Good malt mouth feel with hop character, dry and bitter finish with delicate fruit notes
Comments	Characterful bitter named after founder of the brewery

CLARK'S TRADITIONAL

OG 1038°
Ingredients: pale malt, crystal
malt (4%), chocolate malt
(1%), priming sugar.
Challenger hops

TASTING NOTES

Nose	Rich hop resin bouquet with some light fruit notes
Palate	Sweet balance of grain and hop in the mouth, good dry finish full of hop character and some citric fruit
Comments	Fine, well-balanced bitter

BURGLAR BILL'S
OG 1044
Ingredients: pale malt, crystal malt (4%), chocolate malt (1%), priming sugar. Challenger hops, also dry hopped

TASTING NOTES

Nose	Powerful bouquet of malt, ripe fruit and hop resin
Palate	Rich fruit and grain in the mouth, deep and intense finish with good hop tingle and fruit notes
Comments	Mellow dark beer with complex aromas and flavours

HAMMERHEAD
OG 1056°
Ingredients: pale malt, crystal malt (4%), chocolate malt (1%), priming sugar. Challenger hops

TASTING NOTES

Nose	Massive attack of malt and fruit
Palate	Fat grain in the mouth with hop balance, deep, rounded fruit and hop finish
Comments	Powerful, vinous strong ale; Clark also brew a Winter Warmer (not tasted)

4 Cropton Brewery

**New Inn, Cropton, Pickering, N. Yorks YO18 8HH
Tel: 07515 330**

Independent
Reception centre Yes (in the pub.) Brewery visits by
arrangement

TWO PINTS BEST BITTER

OG 1042° ABV 4.3%
Ingredients: pale malt and crystal malt. Goldings and
Challenger whole hops

TASTING NOTES

Nose	Fresh inviting hop aroma
Palate	Delicate balance of fruit and hop with light dry finish
Comments	Fine quenching bitter, so named because you will not be satisfied with just one pint!

SPECIAL STRONG BITTER

OG 1062° ABV 6.8%
Ingredients: pale malt and
crystal malt. Goldings and
Challenger whole hops

TASTING NOTES

Nose	Powerful smack of hop and fruit notes
Palate	Rich, rounded, mouth-filling balance of hop and grain with delectable long finish
Comments	A dark beer suggesting a healthy amount of crystal malt. Not as sweet as the gravity suggests. Cropton's beers were brewed first for the New Inn but now have outlets in the free trade.

5   Franklins

**Bilton Lane, Bilton, Harrogate, N Yorks HE1 4DH
Tel: 0423 74328**

Independent
Reception centre No. *Brewery tours* No

FRANKLINS BITTER

OG 1038° ABV 3.9%
Ingredients: pale and dark
malt. Continental hops.

TASTING NOTES

Nose	Inviting hop aroma with fruit notes developing
Palate	Complex chewy balance of fruit and grain with dry, bitter finish
Comments	A distinctive and unusual copper-coloured ale, a good session drink

6 Linfit

The Sair, Lane Top, Linthwaite, Huddersfield HD7 5SG Tel: 0484 842370

Independent; brewery attached to pub with free trade
Reception centre No but beers available in Sair Inn.
Brewery tours Yes

LINFIT MILD
OG 1032° ABV 3%
Ingredients: pale ale malt (87%), roast barley (12%),
flaked barley (1%).
Challenger whole hops

TASTING NOTES

Nose	Light grain aroma
Palate	Pleasant chewy grain with dry finish and chocolate hints
Comments	Quaffable dark mild

LINFIT BITTER
OG 1035° ABV 3.5%
Ingredients: pale ale malt (87%), crystal malt (12%),
flaked barley (1%). Challenger whole hops

TASTING NOTES

Nose	Delicate grain and hop aroma
Palate	Clean, quenching hop and grain with dry bitter finish
Comments	Refreshing session bitter

LINFIT SPECIAL
OG 1041° ABV 4%
Ingredients: pale ale malt (88%), crystal malt (11%),
flaked barley (1%). Challenger whole hops

TASTING NOTES

Nose	Grain and hop aroma, fruit notes developing
Palate	Mouth-filling rounded malt on tongue, dry finish with vanilla notes
Comments	Excellent rich copper-coloured ale

ENGLISH GUINEAS STOUT
OG 1041° ABV 4%
Ingredients: pale ale malt (87%), roast barley (12%), flaked barley (1%). Challenger whole hops

TASTING NOTES

Nose	Promising aroma of hop and roast barley
Palate	Rich nut and hop prickle on tongue, dry, chocolaty finish
Comments	Tasty, chewy stout, less dark and with thinner head than Guinness

OLD ELI
OG 1050° ABV 5%
Ingredients: pale ale malt (90%), crystal malt (9%), flaked barley (1%). Challenger whole hops

TASTING NOTES

Nose	Pronounced grain aroma with rich orange peel notes
Palate	Powerful sweetish smack of malt with light hop balance and dry finish with ripe fruit notes
Comments	Rich fine tasting ale, excellent companion for strong cheese

LEADBOILER
OG 1063° ABV 6%
Ingredients: pale ale malt (92%), crystal malt (7%), flaked barley (1%). Challenger whole hops.

TASTING NOTES

Nose	Rich promise of hop and malt, developing pronounced fruit and jam notes
Palate	Powerful mouth-feel of malt and alcohol, hop finish with complex fruit notes
Comments	Cheering orange coloured end-of-session beer, not too sweet in spite of strength

ENOCH'S HAMMER
OG 1080° ABV 8%
Ingredients: pale ale malt (99%), flaked barley (1%).
Challenger whole hops

TASTING NOTES

Nose	Nose-tickling aroma of hops with ripe marmalade notes
Palate	Vast, shattering attack of malt, orange and lemon peel with memorably long finish of hoppy dryness and fruity astringency
Comments	A straw coloured beer for sipping, a rich and powerful brew named after a leading local Luddite and the weapon he used to wreck machines

XMAS ALE
OG 1080° ABV 8%
Ingredients: pale ale malt (99%), flaked barley (1%),
Thorax for colour. Challenger whole hops

TASTING NOTES

Nose	Light hop and grain aroma, developing fruit notes
Palate	Ripe, mouth-filling balance of malt and fruit, pronounced dry finish with sultana notes
Comments	A fine seasonal ale to keep out the chill. Produced in draught and bottle-conditioned forms

7   Malton Brewery Co Ltd

Crown Hotel, Wheelgate, Malton, N Yorks YO17 0HP Tel: 0653 697580

Independent
Reception centre Yes (small). *Brewery tours* by arrangement

MALTON PALE ALE

OG 1033.8° ABV 3.8%
Ingredients: pale malt and crystal malt. Goldings whole hops

TASTING NOTES

Nose	Fresh and inviting hop aroma
Palate	Light, quenching grain and hop with delicate dry finish
Comments	Excellent quaffing ale, well hopped for the gravity

DOUBLE CHANCE BITTER

OG 1037.8° ABV 4.1%
Ingredients: pale malt and crystal malt. Goldings whole hops.

TASTING NOTES

Nose	Rich assault of Goldings, a hoppy explosion
Palate	Superb balance of grain and light fruit with intense dry finish
Comments	Pale coloured ale with a breathtaking bitter character; a splendid companion for fish dishes

PICKWICK'S PORTER

OG 1041.8° ABV 4.4%
Ingredients: pale malt, crystal malt and black malt.
Goldings whole hops

TASTING NOTES

Nose	Heady aroma of hop and dark malt
Palate	Tart, dry balance of grain, toast and pungent fruit with dry hop and chocolate finish
Comments	A jet black stout full of nutty malt character

OWD BOB

OG 1054.8° ABV 6%
Ingredients: pale malt, crystal malt and black malt.
Goldings whole hops

TASTING NOTES

Nose	Rich aroma of hop, dark chocolate and fruit notes
Palate	Full, complex balance of malt and hop, deep finish with roast and chocolate hints
Comments	A dark ruby coloured strong winter ale

8   North & East Riding Brewers Ltd

Highlander Hotel, 15 The Esplanade, South Cliff, Scarborough, N Yorks Tel: 0723 365627

Independent
Reception centre Yes (in the hotel). *Brewery tours* by arrangement

WILLIAM CLARK'S THISTLE MILD

OG 1034°
Ingredients: Maris Otter pale malt, chocolate malt, crystal malt, black malt, maize and torrefied wheat. Challenger and Stirrion whole hops

TASTING NOTES

Nose	Rich dark malt aromas
Palate	Chewy, nutty grain in the mouth, bitter-sweet finish with dark chocolate notes
Comments	Pleasant, mellow dark mild

WILLIAM CLARK'S THISTLE BITTER

OG 1040°
Ingredients: Maris Otter pale malt, crystal malt, maize and torrefied wheat. Challenger and Stirrion whole hops

TASTING NOTES

Nose	Warm aromas of malt and hops
Palate	Rounded malt in the mouth, deep dry finish with light hop notes
Comments	Lightly hopped Scottish style beer

WILLIAM CLARK'S EXB

OG 1040°
Ingredients: Maris Otter pale malt, crystal malt, maize
and torrefied wheat. Challenger and Stirrion whole
hops

TASTING NOTES

Nose	Pronounced hop and malt aromas
Palate	Strong malt feel offset by hop edge, deep dry finish with some fruit notes
Comments	Hoppier, "English" version of Thistle Bitter

WILLIAM CLARK'S 68

OG 1050°
Ingredients: Maris Otter pale malt, crystal malt,
chocolate malt, black malt, maize and torrefied wheat.
Challenger and Stirrion whole hops

TASTING NOTES

Nose	Ripe hop, dark chocolate and bitter fruit bouquet
Palate	Rich and rounded dark malt in the mouth with good bitter edge, long, intense finish with tart fruit
Comments	Tangy, fruity dark stout; the beers are brewed by the Scots Clark family who have free trade as well as their hotel

9   Robinwood Brewers & Vintners

Robinwood Brewery, Burnley Road, Todmorden, W. Yorks OL14 8EX Tel: 0706 818160

Independent
Reception centre Yes, in Staff of Life pub. Brewery visits by arrangement, evenings only

BEST BITTER

OG 1035° ABV 2.8%
Ingredients: Maris Otter malt
(95%), crystal malt (4%),
chocolate malt (1%).
Whitbread Goldings Variety
whole hops

TASTING NOTES

Nose	Rich hop aroma and light fruit notes
Palate	Refreshing balance of grain and hop, dry finish with dark chocolate hints
Comments	Quenching copper-coloured ale

XB

OG 1046° ABV 3.5%
Ingredients: Maris Otter malt (93.8%), crystal malt (5%), pale chocolate malt (1.2%). Whitbread Goldings Variety whole hops

Nose	Light, appealing hop character, fruit notes developing
Palate	Rich tasting malt-and-grain with deep dry finish and slight chocolate hints
Comments	Amber beer with full body and complex balance

OLD FART or OLD XXXX ALE

OG 1060° ABV 5.4%
Ingredients: Maris Otter malt (74%), crystal (6%),
roast barley (4%), malt extract (16%). Whitbread
Goldings Variety whole hops.

TASTING NOTES

Nose	Powerful hop and rich fruit aroma
Palate	Mouth-filling mix of roast barley, raisins and sultanas with deep dry finish
Comments	Idiosyncratic dark beer with stout-like character.

10   Selby (Middlebrough) Brewery Ltd

131 Millgate, Selby, N Yorks Y08 0LL
Tel: 0757 702826

Independent
Reception centre No. *Brewery tours* No.

BEST BITTER

OG 1036°
Ingredients: pale ale malt
(95%), crystal malt (5%).
Sunshine and Worcester
Goldings Varieties whole
hops.

TASTING NOTES

Nose	Rich, inviting hop and citric aroma
Palate	Sharp, tangy malt and grain with deep bitter finish
Comments	Light, refreshing, clean-tasting session bitter; available in bottled form as "No 1 Ale"

OLD TOM

OG 1066°
Ingredients: pale ale malt (95%), crystal malt (5%).
Sunshine and Worcester Goldings Varieties whole
hops.

TASTING NOTES

Nose	Pungent, tempting, pronounced hop flower and citric fruit aroma
Palate	Rounded, mouth-filling malt and fruit with intense, dry finish
Comments	Strong coppery, distinctive sipping ale

11 John Smith's Tadcaster Brewery

**The Brewery, Tadcaster, N Yorks LS24 9SA
Tel: 0937 832091**

Subsidiary of Courage
Reception centre Yes. *Brewery tours* by arrangement

JOHN SMITHS BITTER or JOHN SMITHS YORKSHIRE BITTER
in the south

OG 1036° ABV 3.8%
Ingredients: pale ale malt, brewing sugar, black malt for colour. Target and Yeoman hop pellets

TASTING NOTES

Nose	Light, delicate hop promise, strong fruit hints developing
Palate	Clean balance of grain and fruit with dry finish
Comments	A distinctive ruby-red session ale with pronounced fruit character

JOHN SMITHS MAGNET
OG 1040° ABV 4%
Ingredients: pale ale malt, brewing sugar, Target and Yeoman hop pellets

TASTING NOTES

Nose	Rich grain and hop with hints of orange peel
Palate	Complex grain and hop in mouth with dry bitter finish and hop and vanilla notes
Comments	A dark ruby beer, well-crafted and potable, goes well with cheese or fish

IMPERIAL RUSSIAN STOUT

(bottle conditioned)

OG 1104° ABV

Ingredients: pale ale malt, amber malt, black malt and brewing sugar. Traditional English hop varieties with "hop rate four times that of average bitter"; this indicates in region of 24lbs of hops per barrel of stout

TASTING NOTES

Nose	Fresh leather and creosote
Palate	Stunningly dry bitter black chocolate on tongue with deep, intense hoppy finish
Comments	Not for the faint-hearted! Brewed every two or three years, matured in oak casks and served in nip bottles, this brown-black ale was first brewed by Barclay Perkins for the Imperial Russian trade in the 19th century. Put the port away and enjoy a glass with your Stilton.

2 Samuel Smith Old Brewery (Tadcaster)

**The Old Brewery, High Street, Tadcaster, N Yorks
LS24 9SB Tel: 0937 832225**

Independent
Reception centre Yes. *Brewery tours* Yes.

OLD BREWERY BITTER

OG 1037° ABV 3.8%
Ingredients: pale ale malt
(91%), crystal malt (9%).
Goldings and Fuggles
whole hops

TASTING NOTES

Nose	Grain and delicate hop aroma
Palate	Full malt and fruit on tongue, light dry finish with vanilla essence notes
Comments	A full-flavoured, oaky bitter

MUSEUM ALE

OG 1048° ABV 5.2%
Ingredients: pale ale malt (90%), crystal malt (10%).
Goldings and Fuggles whole hops

TASTING NOTES

Nose	Rich, inviting earthy grain-and-hop aroma
Palate	Complex balance of malt, light hop and developing fruit, with grainy finish
Comments	A deep amber beer. The head brewer tells me that he has stopped using cane sugar in all his brews as part of a policy of producing beers without additives or preservatives

13 Stocks Doncaster Brewery

33-34 Hallgate, Doncaster S Yorks DN1 3NL
Tel: 0302 328213

Independent
Reception centre No. *Brewery tours* by arrangement

STOCKS BEST BITTER

OG 1037.7°
Ingredients: pale malt
(98.65%), chocolate malt
(1.35%). Fuggles and
Goldings whole hops

TASTING NOTES

Nose	Light hop aroma with faint fruit notes
Palate	Pleasing malt and hop balance with dry finish and dark chocolate hints
Comments	Excellent quenching dark-coloured session bitter

SELECT

OG 1044.7°
Ingredients: pale malt (98.15%), chocolate malt
(1.85%). Fuggles and Goldings whole hops

TASTING NOTES

Nose	Earthy hop aroma with rich fruit notes developing
Palate	Smooth rounded malt in mouth with delicate bitter finish
Comments	Tasty, chewy premium ale

OLD HORIZONTAL

OG 1054.7°
Ingredients: pale malt (97%), chocolate malt (3%).
Fuggles and Goldings whole hops

TASTING NOTES

Nose	Enticing aroma of strong hop and chocolate notes
Palate	Deep, rich balance of grain and dark chocolate with intense dry and nutty finish
Comments	A dark and complex strong ale, a feet-up, sipping beer

4 **William Stones**

Bass Brewing (Sheffield) Ltd, Cannon Brewery, 43 Rutland Road, Sheffield, S Yorks S3 8BE Tel: 0742 349433

Subsidiary of Bass
Reception centre Yes. *Brewery tours* by arrangement

STONES BEST BITTER

OG 1038° ABV 4.1%
Ingredients: Pipkin pale ale malt (80%), glucose syrup (20%) plus minute amount of crystal malt. Goldings, Progress, Challenger, Northdown whole hops with occasional use of Bramling Cross; 1oz of dry hops per barrel

TASTING NOTES

Nose	Fragrant dry hop aroma with light fruit notes
Palate	Delicate malt on tongue with mellow bitter finish
Comments	A delectable straw-coloured bitter, not to be confused with the heavily advertised keg and canned beer of the same name

15 Timothy Taylor & Co Ltd

Knowle Spring Brewery, Keighley W Yorks BD21 1AW Tel: 0535 603139

Independent
Reception centre No. *Brewery tours* No.

GOLDEN MILD
OG 1033° ABV 3.5%
Ingredients: Golden Promise malt, "touch of caramel". Fuggles and Goldings whole hops

TASTING NOTES

Nose	Light, delicate hop and grain aroma
Palate	Sweet malt flavour with short lightly bitter finish
Comments	Quaffable pleasant light mild. "Best Dark Mild" is the same beer with extra caramel; "Bitter" is the same brew without caramel

BEST BITTER
OG 1037° ABV 4%
Ingredients: Golden Promise malt, roasted crystal barley. Kent Goldings Varieties, Worcester Fuggles and Styrian Goldings whole hops

TASTING NOTES

Nose	Delicious fresh hop flower aroma, light fruit notes
Palate	Full and complex grain and fruit with deep dry, nutty finish
Comments	A golden bitter of exceptional quality and drinkability

LANDLORD
OG 1042° ABV 4.3%

Ingredients: Golden
Promise malt (100%).
Styrian Goldings,
Worcester Fuggles, Kent
Goldings whole hops

TASTING NOTES

Nose	Fine, full hop aroma developing orange peel and lemon notes
Palate	Stunning, mouth-filling, multi-layered interweaving of grain and hop with intense hop and fruit finish
Comments	A superb beer of enormous character and complexity that has won three Beer of the Year awards from CAMRA and three Brewex Challenge Cups. A Grand Cru of the beer world. "Ram Tam" is the same brew with added caramel

PORTER
OG 1043°
Ingredients: Golden Promise malt, caramel and
roasted barley. Fuggles whole hops

TASTING NOTES

Nose	Soft hop and grain aroma developing some fruit notes
Palate	Pleasing grain and nut in mouth, dry bitter finish with chocolate notes
Comments	An occasional brew with a smooth creamy appeal.

16   Joshua Tetley & Son Ltd

PO Box 142, The Brewery, Hunslet Road, Leeds W Yorks LS1 1QG Tel: 0532 435282

Subsidiary of Allied Breweries
Reception centre Yes. *Brewery tours* by arrangement

TETLEY MILD

OG 1032° ABV 3.2%
Ingredients: English pale
ale malt, cane sugar (14%),
torrefied barley (10%),
caramel for colour.
Goldings, Zenith,
Challenger, Northdown,
Northern Brewer hop
pellets

TASTING NOTES

Nose	Light hint of hop and grain
Palate	Chewy malt in mouth, dry, nutty finish
Comments	Good tasting, easy drinking dark mild

TETLEY BITTER

OG 1036° ABV 3.6%
Ingredients: English pale ale malt, cane sugar (14%),
torrefied barley (10%), caramel for colour. Goldings,
Zenith, Challenger, Northdown, Northern Brewer
hop pellets

TASTING NOTES

Nose	Stunning assault of hop resin and tart lemon fruit
Palate	Smooth mouth-filling balance of grain and hop with deep, intense dry finish and lingering fruit notes
Comments	A superb tangy bitter

TETLEY IMPERIAL

OG 1042° ABV 4.1%
Ingredients: English pale ale malt, cane sugar (14%),
torrefied barley (10%), caramel for colour. Goldings,
Zenith, Challenger, Northdown, Northern Brewer
hop pellets.

TASTING NOTES

Nose	Rich hop aroma developing strong fruity notes
Palate	Fat grain in mouth, bitter-sweet finish
Comments	A creamy, good-tasting ale

17 T & R Theakston Ltd

**The Brewery, Masham, Ripon, N Yorks HG4 4DX
Tel: 0765 89544**

Subsidiary of Scottish & Newcastle Breweries
Reception centre Yes. *Brewery tours* Yes

BEST BITTER

OG 1038° ABV 3.8%
Ingredients: pale malt,
crystal malt, maize and cane
sugar. Fuggles and other
hops, whole and pellets

THEAKSTON
1827 1977
ALES
150 years of tradition

TASTING NOTES

Nose	Pronounced hop resin and light fruit bouquet
Palate	Delicate bitter-sweet balance in the mouth, light dry finish with good hop character
Comments	Pale bitter with distinctive hop flower character

XB

OG 1046° ABV 4.5%
Ingredients: pale malt, crystal malt, maize and cane
sugar. Fuggles and other hops, whole and pellets

TASTING NOTES

Nose	Spicy hop resin aroma
Palate	Good malt and hop balance with deep dry finish and tart fruit notes
Comments	Rich, rounded fruity bitter, excellent with cheese or pasta dishes

OLD PECULIER

OG 1058° ABV 5.6%
Ingredients: pale malt, crystal malt, maize and cane
sugar. Fuggles and other hops, whole and pellets

TASTING NOTES

Nose	Massive winey bouquet of fat fruit
Palate	Toffee and roast malt in the mouth, deep bitter-sweet finish with delicate hop underpinning
Comments	A famous dark, vinous, "pass the Stilton" old ale

Trough Brewery Ltd

**Louisa Street, Idle, Bradford, W Yorks BD10
Tel: 0274 613450**

Independent
Reception centre No. *Brewery tours* No
Trough was producing two beers, Bitter (OG 1035.5°)
and Wild Boar (OG 1039.5°), both brewed temporari-
ly from malt extract. The company has acquired the
brewing plant from the former Goose Eye Brewery
and is planning three new full-mash beers.

19   S.H. Ward & Co Ltd

**Sheaf Brewery, Ecclesall Road, Sheffield, S. Yorks
S11 8HZ Tel: 0742 755155**

Subsidiary of Vaux
Reception centre Yes. *Brewery tours* by arrangement

DARLEY DARK MILD
OG 1032° ABV 3%
Ingredients: Maris Otter and Triumph pale malt
(89%), chocolate malt, crystal malt, torrefied wheat,
invert sugar. Fuggles and Goldings whole hops

TASTING NOTES

Nose	Tempting aromas of malt and chocolate
Palate	Grain and chocolate in the mouth, short dry finish
Comments	Mellow, good tasting dark mild

DARLEY THORNE BEST BITTER
OG 1037° ABV 3.6%
Ingredients: Maris Otter and Triumph pale malt,
crystal malt, torrefied wheat, invert sugar. Fuggles
and Goldings whole hops

TASTING NOTES

Nose	Light aroma of grain and slight hop
Palate	Malt in the mouth, dry finish with some hop notes
Comments	Easy drinking but undistinguished session ale

SHEFFIELD BEST BITTER
OG 1038° ABV 3.8%
Ingredients: Maris Otter and Triumph pale malt
(94%), caramel, enzymic malt, invert sugar.
Challenger, Fuggles and Target whole hops

TASTING NOTES

Nose	Pronounced malt aroma with light hop notes
Palate	Fat malt in the mouth, rounded bitter-sweet finish
Comments	Distinctively malty ale, yet cleansing and not cloying; a recent new bitter, Kirby Ale (OG 1050°) not tasted

Samuel Webster & Wilsons Ltd

Fountain Head Brewery, Ovenden Wood, Halifax, W Yorks IX2 0TL Tel: 0422 63254

Subsidiary of Grand Metropolitan Brewing
Reception centre Yes. *Brewery tours* by arrangement
*Wilsons beers are brewed for the company's tied estate west of the Pennines

WILSONS ORIGINAL MILD

OG 1030.8° ABV 3%
Ingredients: selected ale malt, crystal malt, brewing barley and maize syrup. Goldings, Northern Brewer, Northdown, Wye Challenger and Wye Target hop pellets

TASTING NOTES

Nose	Light hop and vanilla aromas
Palate	Malt and toffee in the mouth, short dry sweetish finish
Comments	Pleasant, easy drinking but unmemorable mild

WEBSTERS GREEN LABEL

OG 1032° ABV 3.2%
Ingredients: selected ale malt, brewing barley and
maize syrup. Goldings, Northern Brewer,
Northdown, Wye Challenger and Wye Target hop
pellets

TASTING NOTES

Nose	Faint hop aroma
Palate	Light balance of grain and hop with dry bitter finish
Comments	Light session ale

WILSONS ORIGINAL BITTER

OG 1035.8° ABV 3.8%
Ingredients: selected ale malt, crystal malt, brewing
barley and maize syrup. Goldings, Northern Brewer,
Northdown, Wye Challenger and Wye Target hop
pellets

TASTING NOTES

Nose	Hop resin and toffee aroma
Palate	Pronounced grain in the mouth with dry hop and vanilla finish
Comments	A smooth, creamy bitter lacking hop character

WEBSTERS YORKSHIRE BITTER

OG 1035.8° ABV 3.8%
Ingredients: selected ale malt, brewing barley, maize
syrup and caramel for colour. Goldings, Northern

Brewer, Northdown, Wye Challenger and Wye Target hop pellets

TASTING NOTES

Nose	Background aromas of some grain and hop
Palate	Soft vanilla and toffee flavours, dry finish with faint hop notes
Comments	Beer that is a product of a mass market mentality, the Hirondelle of the beer world

WEBSTERS CHOICE

OG 1045° ABV 4.5%
Ingredients: selected ale malt, brewing barley, maize syrup and caramel for colour. Goldings, Northern Brewer, Northdown, Wye Challenger and Wye Target hop pellets

TASTING NOTES

Nose	Malt, hop and fruit bouquet
Palate	Ripe malt in the mouth, deep finish with hop notes and some fruit
Comments	Rounded, mellow bitter

21   Whitbread (Sheffield)

**Exchange Brewery, Sheffield, S Yorks
Tel: 0742 761101**

Subsidiary of Whitbread
Reception centre Yes. *Brewery tours* by arrangement

CHESTER'S BEST MILD

OG 1032° ABV 3.5%
Ingredients: pale malt (70%), chocolate malt (5%),
torrefied wheat (15%), sugar (10%). Hop extract
(75%), Target pellet hops (25%)

TASTING NOTES

Nose	Hints of chocolate and coffee
Palate	Thin, slightly astringent with dry finish and chocolate notes
Comments	A dark, pleasant, quaffable dark mild

CHESTER'S BEST BITTER

OG 1033° ABV 3.6%
Ingredients: pale malt (72%), crystal malt (3%),
torrefied wheat (15%), sugar (10%). Hop extract
(85%), Target pellet hops (15%)

TASTING NOTES

Nose	Yeast and grain, with light fruit notes
Palate	Light balance of grain and hop with dry finish and vanilla notes
Comments	A bitter light in body and colour; both Chester's beers are brewed for the Manchester area

TROPHY

OG 1036° ABV 3.8%
Ingredients: pale malt (70%), crystal malt (5%),

torrefied wheat (10%), sugar (15%). Hop extract
(80%), Target pellet hops (20%), dry hopped with
Goldings

TASTING NOTES

Nose	Inviting aroma of hop and grain
Palate	Good balance of malt, hop and light fruit with dry, nutty finish
Comments	Refreshing amber coloured ale, cask version of the ubiquitous keg Trophy

CENTRAL ENGLAND

The great region of central England, taking in the
pastoral delights of Shakespeare country and the
great power houses of the industrial revolution in
Birmingham and the Black Country, includes the
modern capital of English brewing, Burton upon
Trent. It was in Burton that brewers of world
reknown such as Bass and Worthington developed
the style of beer first called pale ale and better
known today as bitter—hoppy, tangy and
quenching ales that rapidly replaced the darker,
heavier and less refreshing porters and stouts. Only
one Burton brewery, that of Marston, now uses the
town's singular method of brewing, the "union
room" in which fermenting wort gushes from linked
oak casks ("held in union") and circulates over a
bed of yeast in troughs above. Bass, however, still
use a yeast strain developed in their sadly
redundant unions and both Draught Bass and
Marston Pedigree have delicate bouquets with a
hint of apple that belie their impressive gravities.
Mild still has dark roots in the region and a beer
style that met the need of blue-collar workers to
refresh themselves and replace lost energy has
fortunately not matched the decline of the area's
industrial base. Dark, nutty milds from Ansells,
Batham, Bass's Highgate, and Holden, with an
amber version from Banks in Wolverhampton, are
classics of their style.

1 Banks's

Park Brewery, Lovatt Street, Wolverhampton WV1 4NY Tel: 0902 711811

Independent, one half of Wolverhampton & Dudley Breweries
Reception centre Yes. *Brewery tours* by arrangement

BANK'S MILD ALE

OG 1036° ABV 3.5%
Ingredients not revealed

TASTING NOTES

Nose	Delicate hop aroma with fruit notes developing
Palate	Beautiful balance of grain and hop with dry vanilla finish
Comments	A superb, quaffable session mild with appealing amber colour.

BANKS'S BITTER

OG 1038° ABV 3.8%
Ingredients not revealed

TASTING NOTES

Nose	Tempting fresh resin aroma with background fruit notes
Palate	Complex balance of grain and hop with subtle dry finish
Comments	Bitter-sweet beer of great depth and character

2   Bass Brewing (Burton)

**137 High Street, Burton upon Trent, Staffs
DE14 1JZ Tel: 0283 45301**

Subsidiary of Bass
Reception centre Yes. *Brewery tours* contact Bass
Museum (tel as above)

DRAUGHT BASS
OG 1043° ABV 4.4%
Ingredients not revealed

TASTING NOTES

Nose	Complex aroma of hop resin, butterscotch and pronounced sulphur
Palate	Multi-layered mouth feel, pronounced maltiness offset by delicate hop, long polished finish with apple notes
Comments	The most widely available premium cask beer in Britain. Sulphur aromas in Burton beers come from the heavy deposits of gypsum in the soil.

WORTHINGTON WHITE SHIELD
(bottle conditioned)
OG 1051° ABV 5.6%
Ingredients not revealed except Challenger and
Northdown hops

TASTING NOTES

Nose	Spice, pepper and nut bouquet
Palate	Dry malt in the mouth with deep nutty finish and hint of sour fruit
Comments	The classic, original India Pale Ale, a superb beer to drink on its own or with fish and cheese dishes. At the end of the brewing process at Burton the bulk beer is filtered and transferred to Sheffield for bottling, where it is given a "dosage" of

yeast to encourage the second
fermentation in bottle. Pour with care to
avoid the sediment entering the glass.

3 Bass, Mitchells & Butlers Ltd

**Cape Hill Brewery, PO Box 27, Birmingham, West
Midlands B116 0PQ Tel: 021-558 1481**

Subsidiary of Bass
Reception centre Yes. *Brewery tours* by arrangement

M&B MILD
OG 1035° ABV 3.4%
Ingredients not revealed

TASTING NOTES

Nose	Pleasing aromas of chocolate and roasted grain
Palate	Nutty and grainy in mouth with light finish and roast/chocolate hints
Comments	Tasty dark mild of character

M&B BREW XI
OG 1040° ABV 4.1%
Ingredients not revealed

TASTING NOTES

Nose	Light hop resin with hint of pear drops
Palate	Sweet grain in mouth, short malty finish
Comments	Beer with pronounced malt character lacking hop bite

4 Bass Brewing (Wolverhampton)

Springfield Brewery, Grimstone Street, Wolverhampton WV10 1JR Tel: 0902 54551

Subsidiary of Bass
Reception centre Yes. *Brewery tours* Yes

SPRINGFIELD BITTER
OG 1036° ABV 3.5%
Ingredients not revealed

TASTING NOTES

Nose	Grain and fruit aroma
Palate	Malt in the mouth, light dry finish with some hop notes
Comments	Pale coloured bitter with sweetish West Midlands character

CHARRINGTON IPA
OG 1039° ABV 3.6%
Ingredients not revealed

TASTING NOTES

Nose	Pronounced malt aroma with orange fruit developing
Palate	Grain in the mouth, tart, slightly astringent finish
Comments	Brewed for London and the South East, a Bowdlerised version of a once famous London bitter

5 D Batham & Son Ltd

Delph Brewery, Delph Hill, Brierley Hill, West Midlands D75 2TN Tel: 0384 77229

Independent
Reception centre Yes (in Vine pub by brewery).
Brewery tours by arrangement, maximum 10 people

MILD ALE
OG 1036°
Ingredients: Full mash of Golden Promise and Maris Otter blended malt, with caramel for colour. Fuggles and Northdown whole hops in copper, casks dry hopped with Goldings

TASTING NOTES

Nose	Pleasing wafts of hop resins and grain
Palate	Rich chewy balance of malt and nut, with light dry finish
Comments	A lovingly crafted darkish mild, effortlesly drinkable

BEST BITTER
OG 1043°
Ingredients: Full mash of Golden Promise and Maris Otter blended malt, no additives for colour. Fuggles and Northdown whole hops in copper, casks dry hopped with Goldings

TASTING NOTES

Nose	Heady promise of grain and hop flower
Palate	Fine sharp hop prickle in the mouth, intense dry finish
Comments	A straw-coloured delectable and refreshing ale. In winter Batham produces an occasional strong ale, either dark Delph Strong Strong or lighter XXX: "depends on the weather!"

6   Burton Bridge Brewery

23 Bridge Street, Burton upon Trent, Staffs
Tel: 0283 510573/36596

Independent
Reception centre Yes (in Burton Bridge pub at front).
Brewery tours Tuesday evenings by arrangement

XL BITTER

OG 1040° ABV 4%
Ingredients: Maris
Otter pale malt (95%),
crystal malt (5%).
Target and Challenger
whole hops in copper,
casks dry hopped with
Target

TASTING NOTES

Nose	Delicate hop and sulphur aroma
Palate	Mouth filling rich blend of malt and hop with long finish full of earthy blackcurrant notes
Comments	A superb rich clarety brew

BRIDGE BITTER

OG 1042° ABV 4.2%
Ingredients: Maris Otter pale malt (95%), crystal malt (5%), Target and Challenger whole hops in copper, casks dry hopped with Styrian Goldings

TASTING NOTES

Nose	Intense hop and winey aroma
Palate	Rich fruit and grain with a deep dry finish full of sultana notes
Comments	Enormous mouth-filling beer, a pudding ale

PORTER

OG 1045° ABV 4.5%
Ingredients: Maris Otter pale malt (92%), crystal malt
(5%), chocolate malt (3%). Target and Challenger
whole copper hops

TASTING NOTES

Nose	Light hop aroma with hints of chocolate
Palate	Warm biscuit in mouth with dry grainy finish
Comments	A deep brown ale to savour, a fine companion for strong cheese

FESTIVAL ALE

OG 1055° ABV 5.2%
Ingredients: Maris Otter pale malt (94%), crystal malt
(5%), chocolate malt (1%). Target and Challenger
whole copper hops

TASTING NOTES

Nose	Salty, resin aroma
Palate	Powerful mouth-filling maltiness, shatteringly dry finish with vanilla notes and sharp hop prickle
Comments	Superb warming strong ale for sipping or drinking through a rich-flavoured meal.

O.X. (OLD EXPENSIVE)

OG 1065° ABV 6.6%
Ingredients: Maris Otter pale malt (94%), crystal malt
(5%), chocolate malt (1%). Target and Challenger
whole copper hops

TASTING NOTES

Nose	Vinous, port wine aromas
Palate	Massive mouth-filling malt and ripe fruit, deep finish with hop, raisins and sultanas. All are fermented with a yeast strain from the National Yeast Culture Bank and propagated in the brewery

7   Davenports Brewery Ltd

PO Box 353, Bath Row, Birmingham, West Midlands B15 1NB Tel: 021-631 3388

Subsidiary of Greenall Whitley
*The brewery was due to close in August 1989 with production transferred to Shipstone of Nottingham

BEST MILD ALE

OG 1035° ABV 3.2%
Ingredients: Maris Otter pale malt (79%), crystal malt, chocolate malt, caramel for colour. Goldings, Northdown, Challenger and Target pellet hops

TASTING NOTES

Nose	Light grain and hop resin
Palate	Sweet malt with coffee hints, light dry chocolate finish
Comments	Light and drinkable darkish ale

TRADITIONAL BITTER

OG 1038.5° ABV 3.9%
Ingredients: Maris Otter pale malt (72%), crystal malt, barley syrup, cane sugar. Goldings, Northdown, Challenger and Target hop pellets in copper, Styrian whole hops for dry hopping in cask

TASTING NOTES

Nose	Fresh resin hop aroma with light citric fruit developing
Palate	Full refreshing balance of grain and hop, light dry hop and fruit finish
Comments	A pale coloured savoursome bitter

WEM BEST BITTER

OG 1037.5° ABV 3.6%
Ingredients: Maris Otter pale malt (77%), crystal
malt, barley syrup, cane sugar. Fuggles and Goldings
hop pellets

TASTING NOTES

Nose	Light grain and hop aroma
Palate	Malt and light fruit with short dry finish
Comments	Golden coloured sipping bitter

WEM SPECIAL BITTER

OG 1042.5° ABV 4.1%
Ingredients: Maris Otter pale malt (80%), crystal
malt, barley syrup, cane sugar. Fuggles, Goldings and
"other varieties" hop pellets

TASTING NOTES

Nose	Pronounced hop and fruit aroma
Palate	Smooth grain in mouth, good hop finish with fruit notes
Comments	A coppery, smooth, medium strong ale. Both Wem beers are brewed for the tied estate of the former Wem brewery in Shropshire; devotees say the Birmingham brews do not match the originals

8   Everards Brewery Ltd

**Castle Acres, Narborough, Leicester LE9 5BY
Tel: 0533 630900**

Independent
Reception facilities. Brewery tours by arrangement

BURTON MILD*

OG 1033° ABV 3.1%
Ingredients: Maris Otter
pale malt (92%), flaked
maize, caramel for colour.
Fuggles, Challenger and
Goldings hop pellets in
copper, whole hops added
to cask

TASTING NOTES

Nose	Hint of hop resin with toffee notes
Palate	Light malt in mouth, vanilla in short finish
Comments	Pleasant, mellow mahoganny-coloured ale

BEACON BITTER

OG 1036° ABV 3.8%
Ingredients: Maris Otter pale malt (87%), torrefied
wheat, cane sugar. Fuggles, Challenger and Goldings
hop pellets in copper, whole hops added to cask

TASTING NOTES

Nose	Delicate hop aroma
Palate	Chewy grain character in mouth, light dry finish
Comments	An amber ale, light and quaffable

TIGER BITTER*

OG 1041° ABV 4.2%

Ingredients: Maris Otter pale malt (85%), flaked maize, cane sugar, barley wort. Fuggles, Challenger and Goldings hop pellets in copper, whole hops

TASTING NOTES

Nose	Fresh hop aroma with light grain and fruit notes
Palate	Rich malt, tangy hop and fruit in finish
Comments	A bronze coloured, fine tasting bitter

OLD ORIGINAL

OG 1050° ABV 5.2%
Ingredients: Maris Otter pale malt (90%), flaked maize, cane sugar. Fuggles, Challenger and Goldings hop pellets in copper, whole hops added to cask

TASTING NOTES

Nose	Tempting hop aroma developing rich fruit notes
Palate	Fine mouth-filling balance of grain and hop with deep, long dried fruit and resin finish
Comments	Luscious ale with deep brown colour, a fine companion for local cheese or smoked fish

OLD BILL

OG 1070° ABV 7.3%
Ingredients: Maris Otter pale malt (67%), cane sugar. Fuggles, Challenger and Goldings hop pellets

TASTING NOTES

Nose	Pronounced hop and ripe fruit
Palate	Rich balance of sweet malt and hop with dry resin and fruit finish
Comments	A warming strong ale, available from October to January

*Mild and Tiger are currently brewed at the Heritage Brewery in Burton

9 Hansons Brewery

High Street, Dudley, West Midlands
Tel: 0902 711811

Independent, part of Wolverhampton & Dudley
Breweries
Reception centre Yes. *Brewery tours* by arrangement

HANSON'S MILD ALE

OG 1035° ABV 3.5%
Ingredients not
revealed

TASTING NOTES

Nose	Light hop and grain with delicate fruit notes developing
Palate	Tasty grain in mouth, dry finish with vanilla notes
Comments	A dark amber mild of great distinction and quaffability

HANSON'S BITTER or BLACK COUNTRY BITTER

OG 1035° ABV 3.4%
Ingredients not revealed

TASTING NOTES

Nose	Appealing grain, hop resin and light fruit
Palate	Pleasing balance of malt and hop, dry finish with fruit hints
Comments	A well-crafted session beer, noticeably different in palate to Banks's Bitter

10 Hardys & Hansons Ltd

Kimberley Brewery, Kimberley, near Nottingham, Notts NG16 2NS. Tel: 0602 383611

Independent
Reception centre Yes. *Brewery tours* Yes.

KIMBERLEY BEST MILD

OG 1035°
Ingredients not revealed

TASTING NOTES

Nose	Light grain aroma
Palate	Pleasing nut on tongue, light, sweet finish
Comments	Malty, easy drinking dark mild

KIMBERLEY BEST BITTER

OG 1039° ABV 4%
Ingredients not revealed

TASTING NOTES

Nose	Tempting promise of grain and hop
Palate	Fat, chewy grain in mouth, fruit notes in finish
Comments	A distinctive malty ale

11   Heritage Brewery Co

Anglesey Road, Burton upon Trent, Staffs DE14 3PF Tel: 0283 63563

Independent
Reception centre Yes. *Brewery tours* (including Heritage Museum) Yes

HERITAGE BITTER

OG 1045°
Ingredients: pale ale malt, invert sugar, crystal malt. English pellet hops

TASTING NOTES

Nose	Fresh hop resin aroma, fruit notes developing
Palate	Full grain in mouth, deep finish full of hop and fruit character
Comments	A tasty dark amber ale. Heritage produces occasional bottled beers, such as the 1100° Thomas Sykes Old Ale. Also brews for Everards (q.v.).

12   Highgate Brewery Ltd

Sandymount Road, Walsall, West Midlands WS 3AR Tel: 0922 23168

Subsidiary of Bass
Reception centre Yes. *Brewery tours* by arrangement

HIGHGATE MILD
OG 1036°
Ingredients: pale ale malt, crystal malt, sugar syrup, torrefied barley, caramel and black malt for colour. Goldings hops

TASTING NOTES

Nose	Tempting aroma of grain and gentle hop resin, chocolate and coffee notes developing
Palate	Chewy malt and light fruit with dry nutty finish
Comments	A beautifully made luscious dark mild from a brewery that makes just one beer, all in cask form

13   Holdens Brewery Ltd

George Street, Woodsetton, West Dudley, West Midlands DY1 4LN Tel: 0902 880051

Independent
Reception centre No. *Brewery tours* by arrangement

BLACK COUNTRY MILD

OG 1037° ABV 3.6%
Ingredients: Maris Otter pale malt (90-95%), sugar and roasted barley. Fuggles and Goldings whole hops.

TASTING NOTES

Nose	Inviting aroma of grain with wholemeal biscuit notes
Palate	Chewy grain and roast in mouth, dry hoppy finish
Comments	A splendid, tasty dark mild, full of grain and hop character

BLACK COUNTRY BITTER

OG 1039° ABV 3.9%
Ingredients: Maris Otter pale malt (90-95%), Fuggles and Goldings whole hops

TASTING NOTES

Nose	Tempting aroma of hop resin and grain, light fruit notes developing
Palate	Light zesty balance of grain and hop with long dry finish
Comments	A golden bitter of great quality, a fine supping ale

BLACK COUNTRY SPECIAL BITTER

OG 1050° ABV 4.8%
Ingredients: Maris Otter pale malt (90-95%), sugar (5-10%). Fuggles and Goldings whole hops

TASTING NOTES

Nose	Tempting aromas of grain and hop resins with orange notes developing
Palate	Mouth-filling grain and fruit with long dry finish
Comments	A rich and well-balanced strong ale

XL OLD ALE

OG 1092° ABV 10%
Ingredients: Maris Otter pale malt (90-95%), sugar (5-10%), roast barley. Fuggles and Goldings whole hops

TASTING NOTES

Nose	Brimming aromas of grain, hops, orange and banana
Palate	Great fat grain in mouth with roast notes, long, deep finish with hop, dark chocolate and raisins
Comments	Dark, dangerously potable winter warmer, ideal companion for Christmas pudding

14   Holt, Plant & Deakin Ltd

**The Brewery Office, 91 Station Road, Oldbury, Warley, West Midlands B69 4LV
Tel: 021-552 1788**

Subsidiary of Allied Breweries
Reception centre Yes. *Brewery tours* by arrangement
*Mild and Bitter brewed by Tetley Walker of Warrington; information only given for home-brewed ales

MILD
OG 1036°

TASTING NOTES

Nose	Delicate malty aroma
Palate	Light hints of grain and caramel, short dry finish
Comments	Pleasant but unmemorable mild

BITTER
OG 1036°

TASTING NOTES

Nose	Pleasant grain and light hop bouquet
Palate	Light balance of grain and hop, dry finish with some hop notes
Comments	Easy drinking light bitter

HOLTS ENTIRE
OG 1043.5% ABV 4.4%
Ingredients: pale malt, "various special malts" and
wheat flour. Various English whole and pellet hops

TASTING NOTES

Nose	Tempting floral hop nose
Palate	Good balance of grain and hop, mellow dry finish
Comments	A smooth and creamy ale

DEAKINS DOWNFALL

OG 1060° ABV 5.5%
Ingredients: pale malt, "various special malts" and wheat flour. Various English whole and pellet hops

TASTING NOTES

Nose	Spicey, vinous bouquet
Palate	Rich fruit and grain in the mouth, deep dry finish with strong hop and ripe fruit
Comments	Ripe, powerful winter ale

15 Home Brewery Ltd

**Mansfield Road, Daybrook, Nottingham, Notts
NG5 6BU Tel: 0602 269741**

Subsidiary of Scottish & Newcastle Breweries
Reception centre Yes. *Brewery tours* Yes

HOME MILD
OG 1036° ABV 3.6%
Ingredients: pale ale malt
(62%), black malt (8%),
crystal malt, maize, caramel
for colour, priming sugar.
Northdown, Target, Styrian
and Fuggles hop pellets

TASTING NOTES

Nose	Inviting aroma of black chocolate and light hop
Palate	Nutty, chewy grain with dry finish and roast and chocolate hints
Comments	Smooth, easy-drinking dark mild

HOME BITTER
OG 1038° ABV 3.8%
Ingredients: pale ale malt (70%), maize, liquid sugar,
caramel for colour. Northdown, Target, Fuggles,
Styrian hop pellets, dry hopped with whole Goldings

TASTING NOTES

Nose	Fresh appealing promise of hop with slight citric fruit notes
Palate	Pleasing balance of grain and hop bitterness in mouth with delicate dry finish and fruit notes
Comments	A pale coloured brew with good drinkability but with a shade less character since company bought by S&N

16 Hoskins Brewery PLC

**Beaumanor Brewery, Beaumanor Road, Leicester
LE4 5QE Tel: 0533 661122**

Independent
Reception centre Yes. *Brewery tours* Yes

BEAUMANOR BITTER
OG 1039°
Ingredients: limited information only—pale malt,
crystal malt, some sugar. Challenger hops

TASTING NOTES

Nose	Good hop aroma, orange peel notes developing
Palate	Light nutty grain with good dry finish
Comments	Good drinking light coloured ale, pleasant hop and grain balance.

PENN'S ALE
OG 1045°
Ingredients: information as for bitter

TASTING NOTES

Nose	Delicate hop aroma, developing rich fruit notes
Palate	Mouth-filling grain with deep finish and strong hints of nut
Comments	Fine coppery ale, ideal companion for a ploughman's lunch with strong cheese and pickles

PREMIUM
OG 1050°
Ingredients: information as for bitter

TASTING NOTES

Nose	Rich grain, light hop resin, glacé fruit notes
Palate	Mouth-filling chewy malt with short finish
Comments	Pale coloured strong brew short on hop character

OLD NIGEL
OG 1060°
Ingredients: information as for bitter

TASTING NOTES

Nose	Fat vinous appeal
Palate	Powerful attack of grain and fruit with deep bitter-sweet finish
Comments	Deceptively pale coloured, like a German pudding wine. Named after the brewer, thought to be the youngest in the business!

17 Hoskins & Oldfield, North Mills, Frog Island, Leicester. Tel: 0533 532191.
No information received; isolated free trade made tasting impracticable

18   Sarah Hughes Brewery

Beacon Hotel, Bilston Street, Sedgley, Dudley
West Midlands Tel: 09073 3380

Independent
Reception centre Yes (hotel). *Brewery tours* by
arrangement

SARAH HUGHES
MILD

OG 1058° ABV 6°%
Ingredients: pale malt and
crystal malt. Fuggles and
Goldings hops

TASTING NOTES

Nose	Tempting aroma of grain and vinous fruit
Palate	Rich mouth-filling grain and hop, intense dry finish with tannin and fruit
Comments	Superb dark brown beer but hardly "mild". Brewed by John Hughes in refurbished hotel brewery, using his grandmother's recipe. Growing free trade

19   Ind Coope Burton Brewery Ltd

**107 Station Road, Burton upon Trent, Staffs
DE14 1BZ Tel: 0283 31111**

A subsidiary of Allied Breweries
Reception centre Yes. *Brewery tours* Yes

ANSELLS MILD
OG 1036° ABV 3.2%
Ingredients not revealed

TASTING NOTES

Nose	Fresh tempting aromas of chocolate and roast malt
Palate	Rich chewy malt and nut with dry finish and dark chocolate notes
Comments	A superb dark mild, easy drinking and long tasting

ANSELLS BEST BITTER
OG 1037° ABV 3.5%
Ingredients not revealed

TASTING NOTES

Nose	Light grain and fruit aromas
Palate	Grainy in the mouth, sweet finish with hints of roast malt
Comments	A lightly-hopped session beer *Ansells' beers are brewed for pubs in West Midlands and South Wales

ABC BITTER
OG 1037° ABV 3.5%
Ingredients not revealed

TASTING NOTES

Nose	Light hop aroma with fruit notes
Palate	Good malty mouth-feel with dry, hoppy finish
Comments	Pleasant and refreshing bitter with good fruit character brewed for Aylesbury Brewery Co pubs in Chilterns area

BENSKINS BEST BITTER
OG 1037° ABV 3.5%
Ingredients not revealed

TASTING NOTES

Nose	Grain and light fruit aroma
Palate	Light malt in mouth, short finish
Comments	Drinkable but unmemorable beer lacking hop character brewed for Benskins pubs in northern Home Counties

FRIARY MEUX BEST BITTER
OG 1037° ABV 3.5%
Ingredients not revealed

TASTING NOTES

Nose	Light promise of grain and hop with orange peel notes
Palate	Malt in the mouth with some fruit, dry finish
Comments	Session beer short on hop character brewed for Friary Meux pubs south of Thames

HALLS HARVEST BITTER
OG 1037° ABV 3.5%
Ingredients not revealed

TASTING NOTES

Nose	Grain and resin aromas
Palate	Malt and nut in mouth, short dry finish
Comments	Sweetish beer lacking hop character brewed for Hall's pubs in Thames Valley

IND COOPE BEST BITTER
OG 1037° ABV 3.5%
Ingredients not revealed

TASTING NOTES

Nose	Light promise of hop, delicate fruit notes developing
Palate	Light but pleasant malt and hop in mouth, short finish
Comments	Refreshing if unexciting session bitter

IND COOPE DRAUGHT BURTON ALE
OG 1047.5° ABV 4.4%
Ingredients not revealed

TASTING NOTES

Nose	Stunning aromas of grain, rich hop and marmalade fruit
Palate	Great mouth-filling balance of grain and hop with superb, memorably intense finish full of hop and fruit notes
Comments	A magnificent and powerful ale, pungent and full of character, a fine beer for drinking through a meal.

TAYLOR WALKER BEST BITTER
OG 1037° ABV 3.5%
Ingredients not revealed

TASTING NOTES

Nose	Grain on nose with slight hop notes
Palate	Malty in mouth with dry, slightly astringent finish
Comments	Session bitter lacking distinctive hop character

) Lloyds

John Thompson Inn, Ingleby, Stanton-by-Bridge, Derbyshire Tel: 03316 3426/2469

Independent
Reception centre Yes (in the pub). *Brewery tours* by arrangement

JTS XXX or BITTER
OG 1042°
Ingredients: pale malt,
barley syrup. Challenger
hops in copper and cask

TASTING NOTES

Nose	Rich promise of hops, with fruit notes developing
Palate	Rounded balance of grain and hop in the mouth, deep dry finish with ripe fruit
Comments	A superbly balanced beer, full of luscious grain and hop character

VIP

OG 1048°
Ingredients: pale malt, barley syrup, chocolate malt.
Challenger hops in copper and cask

TASTING NOTES

Nose	Powerful hop aromas with hints of dark chocolate
Palate	Fat grain in the mouth with good hop balance, long finish with hints of coffee
Comments	Rich and tasty strong ale; VIP is short for Very Important Pint

SKULLCRUSHER

OG 1065°
Ingredients: pale malt, barley syrup, chocolate malt.
Challenger hops in copper and cask

TASTING NOTES

Nose	Massive wine and ripe fruit
Palate	Mouth-filling deluge of malt and fruit, intense finish with hop, chocolate and sultana
Comments	Fruity winter ale. Brewer Chris Voyce lives in Burton upon Trent and brings fresh supplies of yeast from there every week, giving the beers a slightly tart, salty Burton touch.

21 Mansfield Brewery Ltd

**Littleworth, Mansfield, Notts NG18 1AB
Tel: 0623 25691**

Independent
Reception centre Yes. *Brewery tours* Yes

RIDING DARK MILD
OG 1035°
Ingredients: Maris Otter pale malt, crystal malt
(5–10%). Fuggles hop pellets

TASTING NOTES

Nose	Nut and grain aroma
Palate	Bitter-sweet with dry finish
Comments	A distinctive creamy mild

RIDING TRADITIONAL BITTER
OG 1036°
Ingredients: Maris Otter pale malt (80%), invert sugar
(20%). Fuggles hop pellets, dry hopped with Styrian

TASTING NOTES

Nose	Pronounced dry hop resin aroma
Palate	Rich balance of grain and hop, long dry finish
Comments	Distinctive pale bitter with powerful smack of hops

OLD BAILY
OG 1045°
Ingredients: Maris Otter
pale malt (80%), invert
sugar (20%). Fuggles hop
pellets, dry hopped with
Styrian

TASTING NOTES

Nose	Rich hop aroma and vinous fruit notes
Palate	Fat grain and hop in mouth, long finish full of hop and vanilla character
Comments	Ripe sherry-coloured ale

---

22   Marston, Thompson & Evershed PLC

PO Box 26, Shobnall Road, Burton upon Trent DE14 2BW Tel: 0283 31131

Independent
Reception centre Yes. *Brewery tours* Yes

BORDER MILD

OG 1030° ABV 3%
Ingredients: pale malt
(92%), glucose (5%),
sucrose (3%), caramel
for colour. Fuggles,
Goldings and Worcester
Goldings Variety whole
hops

TASTING NOTES

Nose	Nutty promise of grain
Palate	Tasty, chewy malt in mouth, pleasant dry finish with good hop character
Comments	Good-drinking dark mild

MERCIAN MILD
OG 1032° ABV 3.2%
Ingredients: pale malt (83%), glucose (17%), caramel
for colour. Fuggles, Goldings and Worcester Goldings
Variety whole hops

TASTING NOTES

Nose	Grain, hop resin and fruit notes
Palate	Rich and chewy malt and fruit with dry finish and vanilla notes
Comments	A dark, fruity mild of great character and drinkability

BORDER BITTER
OG 1034° ABV 3.4%
Ingredients: pale malt (95%), glucose (5%)). Fuggles,
Goldings and Worcester Goldings Variety whole hops

TASTING NOTES

Nose	Light aroma of grain and delicate hop
Palate	Smooth, understated balance of malt and hop with dry finish and vanilla notes
Comments	A soft, easy-drinking if unremarkable ale

BURTON BEST BITTER
OG 1036° ABV 3.6%
Ingredients: pale malt (83%), glucose (17%). Fuggles,
Goldings and Worcester Goldings Variety whole hops

TASTING NOTES

Nose	Tempting aromas of hop resins, light fruit and sulphur
Palate	Superb balance of grain and hop with long and delicate hop finish
Comments	A beautifully crafted, subtly deceptive Burton beer

PEDIGREE BITTER

OG 1043° ABV 4.5%
Ingredients: pale malt (83%), glucose (17%). Fuggles,
Goldings and Worcester Goldings Variety whole hops

TASTING NOTES

Nose	Complex bouquet of grain, hop, sour fruit with sulphury notes
Palate	Stunning multi-layered and delicious light assault of malt and hops, with long feathery finish full of delightful hop and apples notes with slight saltiness
Comments	Lightly luscious and free from cloying sweetness despite the gravity. A brilliant achievement. Merrie Monk, sold as a "mild", is Pedigree with added caramel

OWD RODGER

OG 1080° ABV 7.6%
Ingredients: pale malt (73%), crystal malt (10%),
glucose (17%), caramel for colour. Fuggles, Goldings
and Worcester Goldings Variety whole hops

TASTING NOTES

Nose	Toast, grain, hops and coffee essence aromas
Palate	Enormous impact of grain and fruit, long bitter-sweet finish with sultana and raisin notes
Comments	A rich and fruity barley wine to be treated with reverence. Fine companion for strong cheese

23 Parish Brewery

Stag and Hounds, Burrough on the Hill, Leicester-shire LE14 2JQ Tel: 066477 781/375

Independent
Reception centre Yes. *Brewery tours* Yes

PARISH BITTER

OG 1038° ABV 3.6%
Ingredients: pale ale
malt (90%), crystal
(4%), wheat (4%),
sugar. Fuggles,
Goldings and
Bramling Cross
whole hops

TASTING NOTES

Nose	Inviting aromas of grain and hop
Palate	Good balance in mouth of malt and hop with quenching dry finish
Comments	Tasty copper-coloured ale

POACHERS ALE

OG 1060° ABV 5.5%
Ingredients: pale ale malt (90%), crystal malt (4%),
wheat (4%), dark sugar. Fuggles, Goldings and
Bramling Cross whole hops

TASTING NOTES

Nose	Powerful assault of grain, hop and vinous fruit
Palate	Mouth-filling sweet malt and orange peel with intense finish of hop and fruit
Comments	A staggering ale in every sense; good with Stilton or venison

BAZ'S BONCE BLOWER
OG 1110° ABV 11%
Ingredients: pale ale malt (90%), crystal malt (4%),
wheat (4%), black malt, black syrup and dark sugar.
Fuggles, Goldings and Bramling Cross whole hops

TASTING NOTES

Nose	Whole fields of hops and grain clamber out of the glass, with dark chocolate notes
Palate	Hoppy port wine in mouth, tremendous "length" of malt, hops, chocolate, nuts and raisins
Comments	A brown-black ale heavy in alcohol; try it in a wine glass. *Parish began as a home-brew pub but now has substantial free trade

24 Premier Ales Ltd

The Brewery, Mill Race Lane, Stourbridge, West Midlands DY8 1JN Tel: 0384 442040

Independent
Reception centre Yes. *Brewery tours* Yes

OLD MERLIN MILD
OG 1039° ABV 3.5%
Ingredients: pale ale malt, dark sugars and caramel. Goldings and Styrian whole and pellet hops

TASTING NOTES

Nose	Delicate aromas of hop resins and fruit
Palate	Pleasing chewy malt in mouth with light dry finish and faint fruit notes
Comments	A smooth, easily drinkable dark brown ale

KNIGHTLY BITTER
OG 1044° ABV 4.5%
Ingredients: pale ale malt, lager malt, crystal malt. Challenger, Target and Hallertau Styrian whole and pellet hops

TASTING NOTES

Nose	Fresh, appealing hop aromas
Palate	Delightful light balance of malt and hop, dry polished finish with faint toffee notes
Comments	A pale amber brew, top-fermented but, as ingredients show, some lager characteristics

KNIGHT PORTER
OG 1040° ABV 3.7%
Ingredients: pale malt, roasted barley, dark sugar, flaked barley. Goldings hop pellets

TASTING NOTES

Nose	Hop and roast barley aromas
Palate	Bitter-sweet balance in mouth with nut notes from roast grain, good finish with hop and chocolate hints
Comments	A ruby-coloured ale with pleasing roast barley character

BLACK KNIGHT STOUT

OG 1050° ABV 5.2%
Ingredients: pale ale malt, roasted barley, flaked barley and dark sugars. Challenger hop pellets

TASTING NOTES

Nose	Nutty aromas of roasted grain and hop
Palate	Smooth malt and hop balance with dry finish and nut and fruit notes
Comments	A fine jet-black stout, silkily drinkable

MAIDEN'S RUIN

OG 1074° ABV 7%
Ingredients: pale ale malt, wheat malt and light sugars. Challenger, Target and Styrian whole and pellet hops

TASTING NOTES

Nose	Powerful attack of hop resin and vinous fruit
Palate	Rich mouth-filling balance of malt and hop with a long finish full of hop, gooseberry and sultana notes
Comments	A dark, fruity strong ale, a good companion for strong-flavoured food

25   Ruddles Brewery Ltd

**Langham, Oakham, Leicestershire LE15 7JD
Tel: 0572 756911**

Subsidiary of Grand Metropolitan Brewing
Reception centre Yes. *Brewery tours* by arrangement

RUDDLES BEST BITTER

OG 1038° ABV 3.8%
Ingredients: pale ale
malt (86%), crystal
malt (4%), syrup
(10%). Fuggles,
Goldings, Challenger
and Bramling Cross
whole hops

TASTING NOTES

Nose	Hop aroma developing strong sultana fruit notes
Palate	Malt in the mouth, short dry finish with pronounced fruit notes
Comments	A rich amber but slightly cloying bitter

RUDDLES COUNTY

OG 1050° ABV 5%
Ingredients: Premium Ale Malt (85%), crystal malt
(4%), syrup (11%). Goldings, Challenger,
Northdown and Bramling Cross whole hops

TASTING NOTES

Nose	Powerful promise of hop and winey fruit
Comments	Mouth-filling and complex balance of grain, fruit and hop with deep, rounded dry fruit finish
Comments	A rich and tasty ale, fine companion for a tangy ploughman's lunch; winner of many Brewex awards

26   James Shipstone & Sons Ltd

Star Brewery, New Basford, Nottingham NG7 7FN
Tel: 0602 785074

Subsidiary of Greenall Whitley
Reception centre No. *Brewery tours* No

MILD ALE

OG 1034° ABV 3.6%
Ingredients: Otter or
Triumph best mild malt
(85%), invert sugar
(15%), crystal malt,
caramel for colour.
Fuggles and Goldings hop
pellets in copper, whole
Goldings for dry hopping

TASTING NOTES

Nose	Light, delicate aromas of hop and slight fruit
Palate	Sweet malt in the mouth, short finish with good hop character
Comments	A pleasant, smooth drinking medium dark mild

BITTER

OG 1037° ABV 4%
Ingredients: Otter or Triumph best pale ale malt
(93%), invert sugar (7%), crystal malt. Fuggles and
Goldings hop pellets in copper, whole Goldings for dry
hopping

TASTING NOTES

Nose	Pronounced hop aroma with slight sulphur notes
Palate	Good balance of malt and grain, rich deep finish with some fruity astringency
Comments	A pale, uncompromising bitter with Burton characteristics

27   Titanic Brewery

1 Dain Street, Middleport, Burslem, Stoke-on-Trent, Staffs ST6 3LE Tel: 0782 823447

Independent
Reception centre Travellers Rest, Newcastle Street.
Brewery tours Yes

BEST BITTER

OG 1036°
Ingredients: pale malt
(97%), flaked wheat
(3%). Goldings and
Fuggles whole hops,
hop pellets for dry
hopping in cask

TASTING NOTES

Nose	Appealing aromas of hop resin
Palate	Refreshing and sharp in mouth, good dry, hoppy finish
Comments	Light pale bitter, a lovely palate-cleansing brew

TITANIC PREMIUM

OG 1042°
Ingredients: Maris Otter pale malt (95%), flaked wheat (5%). Goldings and Fuggles whole hops, hop pellets for dry hopping in cask

TASTING NOTES

Nose	Rich hop resin aromas
Palate	Smooth balance of grain and hop in mouth, long dry finish with citric notes
Comments	Fine refreshing pale bitter

CAPTAIN SMITH'S STRONG ALE

OG 1050°
Ingredients: Maris Otter pale malt (90%), glucose
syrup (5%), flaked wheat (5%). Goldings whole hops

TASTING NOTES

Nose	Tempting fruit and hop aromas
Palate	Much fruit and malt in mouth balanced by deep dry finish
Comments	A dark and potable beer, named in honour (sic) of the captain of the Titanic

CHRISTMAS ALE

OG 1080°
Ingredients: Maris Otter pale malt (85%), glucose
syrup (10%), flaked wheat (5%). Fuggles whole hops

TASTING NOTES

Nose	Heady promise of fruit and liquorice
Palate	Powerful punch of fruit and grain, rich sweet finish
Comments	Dark, sweet occasional ale, described by the brewer as "knock- out drops"

28 Wood Brewery Ltd

**Wistanstow, Craven Arms, Shropshire SY7 8DG
Tel: 0588 672523**

Independent
Reception centre Yes (Plough Inn at front). *Brewery tours* by arrangement

WOOD'S PARISH BITTER

OG 1040°
Ingredients: Premium
pale alc malt (96%),
crystal malt (4%). Fuggles
in copper, dry hopped
with whole Goldings

TASTING NOTES

Nose	Rich, appealing hop resin aromas
Palate	Clean, quenching balance of malt and hop, long finish full of hop flower depth
Comments	A light coloured, superbly drinkable and refreshing bitter

WOOD'S SPECIAL BITTER

OG 1043°
Ingredients: Premium pale ale malt (91%), crystal malt (9%). Fuggles whole hops

TASTING NOTES

Nose	Complex bouquet of hop, grain and fruit
Palate	Fat grain in mouth with dry finish and deep hop, fruit and nut notes
Comments	A russet-coloured ale of great distinction, multi-layered and memorable

WOOD'S WONDERFUL
OG 1050°
Ingredients: Premium pale ale malt (92%), crystal (7%), chocolate malt (1%). Fuggles in copper, whole Goldings for cask hopping

TASTING NOTES

Nose	Great attack of hop flower and jammy fruit
Palate	Generous mouth-filling malt and fruit, deep dry, slightly tannic finish
Comments	Wonderful indeed! A powerful ruby brew of memorable complexity

WOOD'S CHRISTMAS CRACKER
OG 1060°
Ingredients: Premium pale ale malt (83%), crystal malt (16%), chocolate malt (1%). Fuggles in copper, whole Goldings hops for cask hopping

TASTING NOTES

Nose	Enormous fortissimo of hops, raisins and sultanas
Palate	Rich and vinous in the mouth, intense finish rich with hop, dark chocolate, coffee and fruit notes
Comments	A dark ruby winter brew; drink it with Christmas pudding or use it in the mix! *Wood's began life as a pub-brewery but now has substantial free trade. Asked if the brewery used ingredients other than malt, Mr Wood replied "Indeed not!"

29 Wye Valley Brewery

69 St Owen Street, Hereford, Hereford & Worcester HR1 2JQ Tel: 0432 274968

Independent
Reception centre Yes (in Lamb Hotel). *Brewery tours* Yes

HEREFORD BITTER

OG 1037°
Ingredients: pale malt (92%), crystal malt (8%).
Target whole hops

TASTING NOTES

Nose	Inviting hop and slight citric aromas
Palate	Good, refreshing balance of grain and hop with hop flower finish
Comments	A golden ale with a delightfully quenching taste

HPA

OG 1040°
Ingredients: pale malt (97%), crystal malt (3%).
Target whole hops

TASTING NOTES

Nose	Pleasing balance of grain and hop
Palate	Creamy balance of malt and hop bitterness with long dry finish and vanilla notes
Comments	A delectable, good drinking pale bitter

HEREFORD SUPREME BITTER

OG 1043°
Ingredients: pale malt (88%), crystal malt (12%).
Target whole hops

TASTING NOTES

Nose	Zesty hop and grain aromas, fruit developing
Palate	Rich fruit and malt in mouth, deep finish with long hop character and attractive hints of vanilla and sultana
Comments	A dark golden beer with many layers of attractive taste

BREW 69

OG 1055°
Ingredients: pale malt (95%), crystal malt (5%).
Target whole hops

TASTING NOTES

Nose	Rich, aromatic promise of malt and fruit, hop notes
Palate	Mouth-filling fruit and grain, deep finish with hop prickle and fat fruit
Comments	A deceptively pale but powerful barley wine; a fine night cap *Wye Valley began as a home-brew pub and now has growing free trade

EASTERN ENGLAND

East Anglia is the major barley growing region of Britain. Its proximity to the sea means that it produces maritime barley varieties that are considered to be ideal for malting and brewing. Beers from Eastern England are generous and rounded in palate but any sweetness is offset by good hop rates; the end results are ales of great complexity and depth. The region has a less happy record where brewery survival is concerned. Norfolk in particular has been ravaged by takeovers and mergers and its capital city, Norwich, now lacks a single functioning brewery: "The Norwich Brewery Company" trunks in beers from other outposts of the Grand Metropolitan empire. Fortunately there is growing choice and variety as the region's independents are joined by small micro breweries producing beers of great quality and finding ready support in the free trade.

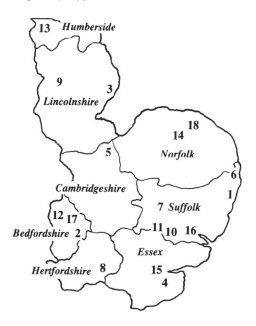

1   Adnams & Company

**Sole Bay Brewery, Southwold, Suffolk IP18 6JW
Tel: 0502 722424**

Independent
Reception centre No *Brewery tours* Trade only

MILD
OG 1034° ABV 3.2%
Ingredients: pale ale malt and crystal malt, priming
sugar. Fuggles and Goldings whole hops

TASTING NOTES

Nose	Light grain and hop aromas
Palate	Soft yet rich malt in the mouth, gentle finish with good chewy malt and hop undertones
Comments	A fine dark and mellow mild

BITTER (BB)
OG 1036° ABV 3.6%
Ingredients: pale ale malt only; "no other cereals".
Fuggles and Goldings whole hops

TASTING NOTES

Nose	Tempting aromas of hop and spice
Palate	Malt underlaid by good hop balance, long bitter-sweet finish with citric and resin notes
Comments	A distinctive, aromatic beer that has lost a slight saltiness since the brewery's well silted up and Adnams now uses the town's water supply

OLD
OG 1042° ABV 4.1%
Ingredients: pale ale and crystal malt. Fuggles and
Goldings whole hops

TASTING NOTES

Nose	Gentle malt aroma with hop notes developing
Palate	Soft malt in the mouth, good chewy grain and hop finish
Comments	Mellow, dark winter beer

EXTRA

OG 1043° ABV 4.3%
Ingredients: pale ale and crystal
malt. Fuggles, Goldings and
Irish Fuggles

TASTING NOTES

Nose	Powerful spicy hop bouquet
Palate	Rich balance of malt and hop resin, deep dry finish
Comments	A ripe, complex strong bitter redolent of hop fields and the North Sea

BROADSIDE

OG 1049° ABV 4.4%
Ingredients: pale ale malt only. Challenger, Fuggles
and Goldings whole hops

TASTING NOTES

Nose	Rich promise of hops and grain
Palate	Fat malt and fruit in the mouth, light dry finish
Comments	A dangerously potable ale that does not "drink its gravity"

TALLY HO

OG 1075° ABV 6.2%
Ingredients: pale ale and crystal malt. Fuggles and
Goldings whole hops

TASTING NOTES

Nose	Rich, vinous, spicy aromas
Palate	Fat malt, fruit and underlying hop prickle in the mouth, long, rounded and complex finish with raisin and sultana notes
Comments	A classic barley wine brewed for the Christmas season

---

2   Banks & Taylor Brewery Ltd

**The Brewery, Shefford, Bedfordshire SG17 5DZ
Tel: 0462 815080**

Independent
Reception centre No. *Brewery tours* by arrangement

SHEFFORD BITTER

OG 1038° ABV 4%
Ingredients: pale malt (95%),
crystal malt (5%).
Challenger, Fuggles and
Goldings whole hops

TASTING NOTES

Nose	Strong hop resin aroma with delicate fruit notes
Palate	Light, clean grain and hop in mouth with quenching finish
Comments	Refreshing and tasty session bitter

SHEFFORD PALE ALE (SPA)

OG 1041° ABV 4%
Ingredients: pale malt (87%), crystal malt (7%),
wheat malt (6%). Fuggles and Goldings whole hops

TASTING NOTES

Nose	Rich grain and hop with citric fruit developing
Palate	Full, rounded grain and hop in mouth, deep dry finish with fruit balance
Comments	Beautifully crafted, rounded ale, fine companion for strong flavoured foods

SHEFFORD OLD STRONG (SOS)

OG 1050° ABV 5%
Ingredients: pale malt (95%), crystal malt (5%).
Fuggles and Goldings whole hops

TASTING NOTES

Nose	Fat wafts of hop resin and ripe, jammy fruit
Palate	Rich, mouth-filling grain with good bitter balance, intense finish with sultana and raisin notes
Comments	Powerful, fruity strong ale, excellent with blue cheese; Shefford Old Dark (SOD) is the same beer with caramel for colour

3 **George Bateman & Son Ltd**

**Salem Bridge Brewery, Mill Lane, Wainfleet
nr Skegness, Lincs PE24 4JE Tel: 0754 880317**

Independent
Reception centre Yes. *Brewery tours* by arrangement

DARK MILD
OG 1033° ABV 3%
Ingredients: pale ale malt
(89%), crystal malt (9%),
wheat (2%), invert sugar,
caramel for colour.
Challenger and Goldings
whole hops

TASTING NOTES

Nose	Biscuit and hazelnut aroma
Palate	Pleasing chewy malt with dry finish and vanilla notes
Comments	Fine example of a tasty dark mild

XB BITTER
OG 1036° ABV 3.8%
Ingredients: pale ale malt (89%), crystal malt (7%),
wheat (4%), invert sugar. Challenger and Goldings
whole hops

TASTING NOTES

Nose	Delicate grain and hop aromas, slight orange fruit notes
Palate	Light, refreshing balance of grain and hop with long dry finish
Comments	A rounded ale of distinction

XXXB BITTER

OG 1048° ABV 4.8%
Ingredients: pale ale malt (87%), crystal malt (10%),
wheat (3%), invert sugar. Challenger and Goldings
whole hops

TASTING NOTES

Nose	Lovely wafts of hop resin and jammy fruit
Palate	Fat malt in the mouth with deep rounded finish and sultana and vanilla notes
Comments	Superb, complex premium bitter, fine companion for ripe cheese

VICTORY ALE

OG 1056°
Ingredients: pale ale malt (90%), crystal malt (5%),
wheat (5%), invert sugar. Challenger and Goldings
whole hops

TASTING NOTES

Nose	Luscious aromas of hop and orange and pear drops
Palate	Full malt in the mouth, intense finish with complex balance of hop bitterness, raisins and vanilla
Comments	A delightful, mellow strong ale, brewed to celebrate the brewery's victory against closure in the mid-1980s

4 Crouch Vale Brewery Ltd

12 Redhills Road, South Woodham Ferrers, Chelmsford, Essex CM3 5UP Tel: 0245 322744

Independent
Reception centre No. *Brewery tours* by arrangement

WOODHAM BITTER

OG 1035.5° ABV 3.7%
Ingredients: pale malt (88%),
wheat malt (7%), crystal
malt (5%). Challenger,
Northdown, Worcester
Goldings Variety,
Progress and East Kent
Goldings whole hops

TASTING NOTES

Nose	Tempting dry hop and grain
Palate	Sharp, quenching balance of malt and hop, light bitter-sweet finish
Comments	Refreshing, well-made light bitter

BEST BITTER

OG 1039° ABV 4.1%
Ingredients: pale malt (94.5%), crystal malt (6.5%).
Challenger, Northdown, Progress, Worcester
Goldings Variety, East Kent Goldings whole hops

TASTING NOTES

Nose	Rich hop aroma with fruit and nut developing
Palate	Exceptionally dry in the mouth with intense bitter finish
Comments	An uncompromisingly tart bitter beer

SAS

OG 1048° ABV 5%

Ingredients: pale malt (88%), wheat malt (7%),
crystal malt (5%). Challenger, Northdown, Worcester
Goldings Variety, Progress, East Kent Goldings whole
hops

TASTING NOTES

Nose	Luscious aromas of grain and hop resins
Palate	Dry grain and hop in the mouth, intense, long bitter finish
Comments	Deceptively light-bodied brew with sharp hop edge

ESSEX PORTER

OG 1050° ABV 5°
Ingredients: pale malt (88%), wheat malt (7%),
crystal malt (5%), roast barley for colour. Challenger,
Worcester Goldings Variety, Northdown, East Kent
Goldings whole hops

TASTING NOTES

Nose	Luscious aromas of roast barley and treacle
Palate	Fat mouth-filling fruit and nutty barley with liquorice notes in the dry finish
Comments	Dark bitter-sweet ale, rich and smooth

WILLIE WARMER

OG 1060° ABV 6.5%
Ingredients: pale malt (95%), crystal malt (5%): 20%
of total extract is sugar. Challenger whole hops

TASTING NOTES

Nose	Biscuity and liquorice aromas
Palate	Powerful mouth-filling roast barley and ripe fruit, rich bitter-sweet finish with hints of fruit and nut
Comments	Powerful sipping strong ale; liable to prosecution under the Trade Descriptions Act

5   Elgood & Sons Ltd

**North Brink Brewery, Wisbech, Cambs PE13 1LN
Tel: 0945 3160**

Independent
Reception centre No. *Brewery tours* No

EB or BITTER
OG 1036° ABV 4.1%
Ingredients: mild ale malt,
wheat, maize, caramel,
invert sugar. Fuggles whole
hops

TASTING NOTES

Nose	Delicate hop aroma
Palate	Ripe fruit in the mouth with dry finish
Comments	Tasty session bitter

GSB
OG 1045° ABV 5.2%
Ingredients: mild ale malt, wheat, maize, caramel,
invert sugar. Fuggles whole hops

TASTING NOTES

Nose	Light hop aroma with some fruit notes developing
Palate	Rich malt and fruit in the mouth, long bitter-sweet finish
Comments	Well-balanced premium ale, goes well with cheese

6   Forbes Oulton Broad Brewery

Unit 20, Harbour Road Industrial Estate, Lowestoft, Suffolk Tel: 0502 587905

Independent
Reception centre No. *Brewery tours* Yes

FORBES BEST BITTER

OG 1046°
Ingredients: 100% malt
mash, no additives, colours
or sugars. "Traditional
varieties" of hops

TASTING NOTES

Nose	Delightful bouquet of hop resins, grain and fruit notes
Palate	Fat malt in the mouth balanced by deep bitter-sweet finish
Comments	Superb all-malt ale from the most easterly brewery in Britain

7   Greene, King & Sons PLC

Westgate Brewery, Bury St Edmunds, Suffolk IP33 1QT Tel: 0284 763222

Independent
Reception centre No. *Brewery tours* Trade only

XX MILD
OG 1031° ABV 3%
Ingredients not revealed

TASTING NOTES

Nose	Light hint of hops and chocolate notes
Palate	Malt in the mouth, pleasant dry finish with chocolate and coffee hints
Comments	A variable beer, sometimes thin but pleasant malt-and- chocolate at its best

GREENE KING IPA
OG 1036° ABV 3.6%
Ingredients not revealed

TASTING NOTES

Nose	Tempting hop aroma with orange fruit developing
Palate	A complex balance of grain, fruit and hop with long estery finish
Comments	A distinctive well-rounded ale, excellent with pub lunch

RAYMENTS BBA (BEST BITTER ALE)

OG 1036° ABV 3.6%
Ingredients: "all malt brew", no further information

TASTING NOTES

Nose	Delicate hop aroma with fruit notes developing
Palate	Good grain and hop balance in mouth, bitter-sweet finish with hints of citric fruit
Comments	Fine session bitter with more hop character than IPA; brewed for the former Rayment's trading area of Hertfordshire and Essex

GREENE KING ABBOT ALE

OG 1048° ABV 5%
Ingredients not revealed

TASTING NOTES

Nose	Powerful aromas of hop resins and ripe fruit
Palate	Enormous attack of fat grain and marmalade fruit, offset by deep hop character. Intense, rich bitter-sweet finish
Comments	The apotheosis of the brewer's art, a strong beer of enormous complexity, any tendency towards sweetness deterred by conditioning over a bed of hops. A superb drink with traditional English fayre

8 McMullen & Sons Ltd

Hertford Brewery, 29 Old Cross, Hertford, Herts SG14 1RD Tel: 0992 584911

Independent
Reception centre Yes. *Brewery tours* by arrangement

ORIGINAL AK
OG 1033° ABV 3.8%
Ingredients: East Anglian pale malt (79%), chocolate malt (1%), maltose syrup (14%), flaked maize (6%). Whitbread Goldings Variety whole hops

TASTING NOTES

Nose	Hop flower and light fruit aromas
Palate	Grain, fruit and delicate hop in mouth, good dry finish with orange peel and faint chocolate notes
Comments	A superb, tasty ale marketed now as a pale ale though its origins are as a light mild

COUNTRY BEST BITTER
OG 1041° ABV 4.6%
Ingredients: East Anglian pale malt (76%), crystal malt (4%), maltose syrup (14%), flaked maize (6%). Whitbread Goldings Variety whole hops in copper and for dry hopping

TASTING NOTES

Nose	Rich, tempting aromas of hop flowers and ripe fruit
Palate	Full, mouth-filling grain and fruit, deep dry finish with pronounced fruit and vanilla notes
Comments	Brilliant balance of grain and hop character, a well-attenuated beer that drinks more than its gravity suggests

CHRISTMAS ALE
OG 1070° ABV 7%
Ingredients: East Anglian pale malt (74%), crystal
malt (4%), maltose syrup (19%), flaked maize (6%),
caramel (in copper: 1%). Whitbread Goldings Variety
whole hops

TASTING NOTES

Nose	Heady aromas of hop and banana
Palate	Vinous in the mouth, intense and prolonged bitter-sweet finish with raisins and sultanas
Comments	Liquid Christmas pudding!

● **Martin Brewery**

**92 High Street, Martin, Lincoln LN4 3QT
Tel: 05267 538**

Independent
Reception centre No. *Brewery tours* by arrangement
("It'll take about three miniutes!")

STANLEY BITTER
OG 1037°
Ingredients: pale malt and crystal malt. Fuggles and
Goldings whole hops

TASTING NOTES

Nose	Rich Goldings promise
Palate	Full grain and hop in the mouth, tart, cleansing finish
Comments	A refreshing golden bitter with a full palate that suggests greater gravity

10 Mauldons Brewery

7 Addison Road, Chilton Industrial Estate, Sudbury, Suffolk CO10 6YW Tel: 0787 311055

Independent
Reception centre No. *Brewery tours* by arrangement

MAULDONS BITTER

OG 1037° ABV 3.3%
Ingredients:
Premium pale ale
malt and crystal malt.
Goldings and
Challenger whole
hops

TASTING NOTES

Nose	Delicate hop aroma
Palate	Good balance of grain and hop with bitter-sweet finish
Comments	Excellent copper-coloured supping bitter

MAULDONS PORTER

OG 1042° ABV 3.7%
Ingredients: Premium pale ale malt, crystal malt and black malt. Goldings and Challenger whole hops

TASTING NOTES

Nose	Pleasing aromas of hop and nut
Palate	Rich nut in the mouth, creamy finish with coffee and chocolate hints
Comments	A ripe-tasting delectable black beer

SQUIRES BITTER

OG 1044° ABV 4%
Ingredients: Premium pale ale malt and crystal malt. Goldings and Challenger whole hops

TASTING NOTES

Nose	Ripe aromas of hop and fruit
Palate	Rich rounded grain in the mouth with bitter-sweet finish
Comments	A fine coppery ale with good balance; excellent with food

SUFFOLK PUNCH

OG 1050° ABV 4.5%
Ingredients: Premium pale ale malt and crystal malt.
Goldings and Challenger whole hops

TASTING NOTES

Nose	Powerful wafts of hop resins and developing fruit
Palate	Ripe grain and jammy fruit with a deep dry finish
Comments	A powerful deep copper ale with great fruit appeal

BLACK ADDER

OG 1055° ABV 5.2%
Ingredients: Premium pale ale malt, crystal malt and
black malt. Goldings and Challenger whole hops

TASTING NOTES

Nose	Roast and nut aromas
Palate	Fine fruity balance of hop and dark malt in the mouth, intensely long dry finish with coffee and nut notes
Comments	Grainy, chewy, memorably tasty strong stout

11   Nethergate Brewery Co Ltd

11-13 High Street, Clare, near Sudbury, Suffolk CO10 8NY Tel: 0787 277244

Independent
Reception centre No. *Brewery tours* Yes

NETHERGATE BITTER
OG 1039° ABV 4.1%
Ingredients: Maris Otter pale malt (88.71%), wheat flour (4.93%), crystal malt (4.93%), black malt (1.43%). Goldings pellets and Fuggles whole hops

TASTING NOTES

Nose	Light aromas of hop, grain and some fruit notes
Palate	Rich and rounded balance of malt and hop, deep finish with fruit hints
Comments	A succulent coppery ale with a full palate that suggests a greater gravity. Excellent with fish and cheese

OLD GROWLER
OG 1055° ABV 5.8%
Ingredients: Maris Otter pale malt (85.34%), wheat flour (3.41%), crystal malt (8.53%), black malt (2.72%). Goldings pellets and Fuggles whole hops

TASTING NOTES

Nose	Light aromas at first, developing hop and liquorice
Palate	Full bitter-sweet in mouth with deep finish and hints of liquorice and black chocolate
Comments	Dark and smooth porter ale

12 Nix Wincott Brewery

Three Fyshes Inn, Bridge Street, Turvey, Bedford MK43 8ER

Independent
Reception centre Yes (in pub). *Brewery tours* During licensed hours

TWO HENRYS BITTER

OG 1039° ABV 3.85%
Ingredients: pale malt (90%), crystal malt (10%). Fuggles and Goldings whole hops

NIX WINCOTT BREWERY

Two Henry's Bitter

TASTING NOTES

Nose	Rich hop aroma with nutty hints
Palate	Rounded malt in mouth, long dry finish with hop and nut appeal
Comments	An amber ale with good drinkability and balance

OLD NIX

OG 1056.5° ABV 5.7%
Ingredients: pale malt (94.4%), crystal malt (5.6%). Fuggles and Goldings whole hops

TASTING NOTES

Nose	Powerful promise of grain and fruit
Palate	Ripe malt and hop in the mouth, intense finish with hop, raisins and sultana
Comments	A pale coloured, robust strong beer, splendid with tangy cheese

13   Old Mill Brewery

Mill Street, Snaith, near Goole, Humberside DN14 9HS Tel: 0405 861813

Independent
Reception centre No. *Brewery tours* No

TRADITIONAL MILD

OG 1034°
Ingredients: pale malt, crystal malt, pale chocolate malt, black malt. Fuggles, Goldings and Styrian hop pellets

TASTING NOTES

Nose	Light aromas of hop and liquorice
Palate	Pleasant chewy malt in mouth, dry finish with dark chocolate hints
Comments	Dark, tasty and nutty mild

TRADITIONAL BITTER

OG 1037°
Ingredients: pale malt and crystal malt. Fuggles, Goldings and small amount of Styrian hop pellets

TASTING NOTES

Nose	Tempting hop and delicate fruit aromas
Palate	Ripe, balanced grain and hop in mouth, clean dry finish
Comments	A rich amber beer with a full palate suggesting greater gravity

BULLION
OG 1044°
Ingredients: pale malt, crystal malt and pale chocolate malt. Goldings, Fuggles and some Styrian hop pellets

TASTING NOTES

Nose	Heady wafts of hop resins and ripe fruit
Palate	Mouth-filling malt with hop undertones, deep bitter-sweet finish with coffee and raisin notes
Comments	Superb, quaffable dark amber ale, winner of three awards at the Great British Beer Festival

4 Reepham Brewery

**1 Collers Way, Reepham, Norfolk NR10 4SW
Tel: 0603 871091**

Independent
Reception centre No. *Brewery tours* No

RAPIER PALE ALE
OG 1044° ABV 4.5%
Ingredients: pale malt and crystal malt (95%), wheat (1%), barley syrup (4%). Fuggles and Goldings whole hops

TASTING NOTES

Nose	Heady bouquet of malt and hops
Palate	Full, rich grain in the mouth, deep dry finish
Comments	Ripe, rounded good-drinking pale golden bitter

SMUGGLERS STOUT

OG 1047° ABV 4.8%
Ingredients: pale malt (84%), crystal malt (8%), black and chocolate malt (4%), wheat (4%). Fuggles and Goldings whole hops

TASTING NOTES

Nose	Burnt toast, rich grain and hop aromas
Palate	Deep bitter flavours of charred malt, long intensely dry finish with coffee notes
Comments	Red-black stout with deep, complex flavours

BREWHOUSE ALE

OG 1055° ABV 5.8%
Ingredients: pale malt and crystal malt (90%), wheat (5%), barley syrup (5%). Fuggles and Goldings whole hops

TASTING NOTES

Nose	Hearty bouquet of sweet malt and hop resin
Palate	Full mouth-filling sweet grain with long dry finish with fruit notes
Comments	Fine, ripe ruby-red strong ale

15   T.D. Ridley & Sons Ltd

Hartford End Brewery, Chelmsford, Essex CM3 1JZ Tel: 0371 820316

Independent
Reception centre Yes (sample room). *Brewery tours* by arrangement

MILD or XXX
OG 1034° ABV 3.5%
Ingredients: Best pale ale malt, crystal malt, chocolate malt, caramel, invert sugar. Fuggles and Goldings whole hops

TASTING NOTES

Nose	Delicate hop aroma
Palate	Mellow nut in mouth, dry finish
Comments	Pleasant dark ruby mild

BITTER or PA
OG 1034° ABV 3.5%
Ingredients: Best pale ale malt, crystal malt, invert sugar. Fuggles and Goldings whole hops

TASTING NOTES

Nose	Aromatic hop aroma with citric notes
Palate	Tangy quenching balance of grain, hop and fruit in mouth, exceptionally long, dry finish
Comments	A stunning, exceptional golden bitter: British beer at its best

16   Tolly Cobbold

**Tollemache & Cobbold Breweries Ltd
PO Box 5, Cliff Brewery, Ipswich, Suffolk IP3 0AZ
Tel: 0473 56751**

Independent, owned by Brent-Walker PLC
*Brewery closed July 1989; production transferred to
Cameron of Hartlepool; beer range and palates liable
to change
Reception centre Yes. *Brewery tours* by arrangement

MILD
OG 1031°
Ingredients not revealed

TASTING NOTES

Nose	Malty with faint chocolate hints
Palate	Grain in the mouth, short dry finish
Comments	A sweetish dark ale

BITTER
OG 1034°
Ingredients not revealed

TASTING NOTES

Nose	Pungent hop resin aroma with orange peel hints
Palate	Complex balance of malt in mouth and intense dry finish
Comments	A tasty, tangy bitter of distinction

ORIGINAL
OG 1037°
Ingredients not revealed

TASTING NOTES

Nose	Rounded aromas of hop, grain and ripe fruit
Palate	Full and bitter-sweet in the mouth, deep dry finish with fruit hints
Comments	Well-flavoured Anglian ale, good with a ploughman's lunch

XXXX
OG 1046°
Ingredients not revealed

TASTING NOTES

Nose	Heady hop, grain and marmalade fruit
Palate	Succulent balance of ripe fruit and hop bitterness, finish has winey, almost Cognac notes
Comments	A good member of the strong, fruity strong ales typical of the region. A winter brew, Old Strong, has the same gravity, but was not available for tasting

17   Charles Wells

Havelock Street, Bedford, Beds MK40 4LO
Tel: 0234 65100

Independent
Reception centre Yes. *Brewery tours* by arrangement

EAGLE BITTER
OG 1035° ABV 3.6%
Ingredients: pale malt (80-85%), crystal malt.
Challenger and Goldings hops

TASTING NOTES

Nose	Aromatic floral hop bouquet
Palate	Light and refreshing balance of grain and hop with dry finish and orange peel notes
Comments	Superbly balanced, quenching tawny ale

BOMBARDIER
OG 1042° ABV 4.2%
Ingredients: pale malt ("almost
100%"), crystal malt.
Challenger and Goldings hops

TASTING NOTES

Nose	Rich, earthy hop resin bouquet
Palate	Ripe malt in the mouth with good hop balance, intensely dry finish with blackcurrant notes
Comments	Deep copper-coloured, finely balanced ale

18 **Woodforde's Norfolk Ales**

**Broadland Brewery, Woodbastwick, Norwich
Norfolk NR13 6SW Tel: 0603 720353**

Independent
Reception centre/brewery tours from 1990

BROADSMAN BITTER

OG 1036° ABV 3.7%
Ingredients: 100% pale
and crystal malt.
Goldings and Stirrion
whole hops

TASTING NOTES

Nose	Delicate, appealing hop bouquet
Palate	Cleansing balance of hop and grain, light dry finish
Comments	Excellent light session bitter

WHERRY BEST BITTER

OG 1039° ABV 4%
Ingredients: 100% pale and crystal malt. Goldings and
Stirrion whole hops

TASTING NOTES

Nose	Rich malt and hop aroma
Palate	Fat malt in the mouth offset by good hop edge, with sharp, tangy finish
Comments	Ripe, complex pale bitter—"and end of the evening beer" says Michael Jackson

NORFOLK PORTER

OG 1042° ABV 4.3%

Ingredients: pale, crystal, chocolate malt and roasted barley. Goldings and Stirrion whole hops, also dry hopped

TASTING NOTES

Nose	Bewitching aromas of dark grain and rich hop
Palate	Bitter-sweet dark malt in the mouth, long dry finish with roast coffee and bitter fruit notes
Comments	Rich, dark, deep-tasting beer

PHOENIX XXX
1047° ABV 4.9%
Ingredients: pale, crystal and chocolate malt. Goldings and Stirrion whole hops

TASTING NOTES

Nose	Deep, complex aromas of hop and developing fruit
Palate	Rounded malt in the mouth, deep fruity finish with pear drop character
Comments	Strong, mellow and complex ale

HEAD CRACKER
OG 1069° ABV 7%
Ingredients: 100% pale ale malt. Goldings and Stirrion whole hops

TASTING NOTES

Nose	Heady bouquet of powerful hop resin, malt and ripe fruit
Palate	Rich, intense mouth-feel of grain and tangy hop, deep dry finish with complex tangy fruit
Comments	Superb and deceptively pale strong sipping ale

THAMES VALLEY

It would be wrong to consider the breweries of the Thames Valley as living in the shadow of the brewing traditions of the ever-burgeoning capital of London. "Country beer" may not be a style as such but it suggests a slow, ruminative, straw-in-the-mouth approach to life which has little truck with modern, fast city attitudes. The "we've been doing things this way for centuries" approach to life is epitomised by Oxford where breweries (now reduced to one) developed from ancient university brew houses established long before the hop had made its controversial arrival in England. The general taste of Thames Valley beers is something of an amalgam of the full, fruity grain of nearby East Anglia and the quenching hoppy edge of beers south of the capital. And one of the delights of good ale in the region is the profusion of genuine and unspoilt rural pubs in which to savour them.

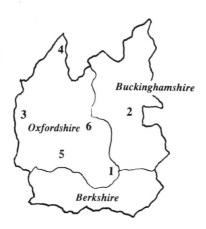

1 W. H. Brakspear & Sons PLC

**The Brewery, New Street, Henley-on-Thames
Oxon RG9 2BU Tel: 0491 573636**

Independent
Reception centre Yes. *Brewery tours* by arrangement

MILD or XXX
OG 1030° ABV 2.8%
Ingredients: Maris Otter
pale malt, crystal malt,
black malt, invert sugar.
Fuggles and Goldings
whole hops

TASTING NOTES

Nose	Light hop and nut aromas
Palate	Pleasing chewy grain in the mouth, dry finish with chocolate notes
Comments	Tasty, good drinking dark mild

BITTER or PA
OG 1035° ABV 3.4%
Ingredients: Maris Otter pale malt, crystal malt, black malt, invert sugar. Fuggles and Goldings whole hops

TASTING NOTES

Nose	Wholemeal biscuit and orange peel aromas
Palate	Full-flavoured grain and hop flower in mouth, delicate dry finish with massive hop flower character
Comments	A superb, beautifully-crafted, satisfying and refreshing bitter—"the best beer in southern England", says John Mortimer

SPECIAL BITTER or SPA

OG 1049° ABV 4%
Ingredients: Maris Otter pale malt, crystal malt, black
malt, invert sugar. Fuggles and Goldings whole hops

TASTING NOTES

Nose	Rich grain, hop and fruit aromas
Palate	Ripe, rounded malt and fruit in the mouth, intense bitter-sweet finish with orange and banana notes
Comments	A coppery, tranquil ale, ideal with a hunk of good bread and strong cheese. The winter brew Old or XXXX is the same beer with added colour

2   Chiltern Brewery

Nash Lee Road, Terrick, Aylesbury, Bucks HP17 0TQ Tel: 029 661 3647

Independent
Reception centre Yes. *Brewery tours* by arrangement

CHILTERN ALE
OG 1036°
Ingredients: pale malt, crystal malt, invert sugar. Challenger, Fuggles and Goldings whole hops

TASTING NOTES

Nose	Light bouquet of hop resin and hint of nut
Palate	Tart balance of grain and hop with long dry finish and fruit notes
Comments	Tangy, cleansing light bitter

BEECHWOOD BITTER
OG 1041°
Ingredients: pale malt, crystal malt, invert sugar. Challenger, Fuggles and Goldings whole hops

TASTING NOTES

Nose	Warm aromas of malt, Goldings and nut grain
Palate	Hearty malt in the mouthy, deep dry finish with fruit and nut notes
Comments	Rounded, balanced ale, cleansing and quaffable. Chiltern also brews a bottle-conditioned Three Hundreds Old Ale (1050°); not tasted

3 Glenny Brewery Co

Two Rivers Brewery, Station Lane, Witney, Oxon OX8 6BH Tel: 0993 702574

Independent
Reception centre No. *Brewery tours* No

WITNEY BITTER
OG 1036° ABV 3.9%
Ingredients: Premium pale malt (89%), crystal malt (4%), chocolate malt (0.5%), flaked barley (6.5%). Progress whole hops in copper, casks dry hopped with Hallertau

TASTING NOTES

Nose	Fresh hop resin aroma
Palate	Light, tasty balance of hop and grain with dry, hoppy finish
Comments	Deep copper-coloured, good drinking session bitter

WYCHWOOD BEST
OG 1044° ABV 4.8%
Ingredients: Premium pale malt (96%), crystal malt (3.75%), chocolate malt (0.25%). Progress whole hops in copper, casks dry hopped with Styrian Goldings

TASTING NOTES

Nose	Nostril-tickling wafts of Goldings with grain notes
Palate	Full malt in the mouth with hop balance, rich fruity finish
Comments	A rounded, light copper ale, the result of three weeks conditioning in the brewery

HOBGOBLIN

OG 1058° ABV 6.5%
Ingredients: Premium
pale malt (92.5%),
crystal malt (4%),
chocolate (0.5%),
flaked barley (3%).
Progress whole hops in
copper, casks dry
hopped with Styrian
Goldings and
Hallertau

TASTING NOTES

Nose	Grain and dark chocolate aromas with good hop notes
Palate	Full and rounded grain in the mouth, deep, dry hop and fruit finish
Comments	Plum coloured strong ale, exceptionally dry as brewed out to a final gravity of 1012°

4   Hook Norton Brewery Co Ltd

**Brewery Lane, Hook Norton, Banbury, Oxon
Tel: 0608 737 210**

Independent
Reception centre No. *Brewery tours* by arrangement

BEST MILD

OG 1032° ABV 2.9%
Ingredients: Maris Otter pale
malt (94%), flaked maize (6%),
caramel for colour. Fuggles,
Goldings and Challenger whole
hops

TASTING NOTES

Nose	Light grain and nut aromas
Palate	Malt in the mouth with good hop finish and some fruit notes
Comments	Distinctive and tasty light mild

BEST BITTER

OG 1036° ABV 3.3%
Ingredients: Maris Otter pale malt (94%), flaked
maize (6%), caramel for colour. Fuggles, Goldings
and Challenger whole hops

TASTING NOTES

Nose	Pronounced hop resin aroma with grain and fruit developing
Palate	Light dry balance of grain and hop with delicate finish and some citric fruit notes
Comments	A distinctive pale bitter with some light fruit complexity

OLD HOOKEY

OG 1049° ABV 4.3%
Ingredients: Maris Otter pale malt (994%), flaked
maize (6%), caramel for colour. Fuggles, Goldings
and Challenger whole hops

TASTING NOTES

Nose	Heady promise of malt and ripe fruit
Palate	Stunning and complex balance of grain, fruit and hop bitterness in the mouth, deep bitter-sweet finish with raisin notes
Comments	A fine old ale: "Treat it with respect" the brewer advises

5   Morland & Co PLC

**PO Box 5, The Brewery, Ock Street, Abingdon,
Oxon OX14 5DD Tel: 0235 553377**

Independent
Reception centre No. *Brewery tours* Yes

BITTER
OG 1035° ABV 4%
Ingredients: pale malt,
crystal malt, brewing sugar.
Challenger and Goldings
whole hops

TASTING NOTES

Nose	Fresh hop flower aroma
Palate	Dry and quenching with a light hoppy finish
Comments	Strong Goldings character makes this a refreshing session beer

OLD MASTERS
OG 1040° ABV 4.6%
Ingredients: pale malt, crystal malt, wheat and
brewing sugar. Challenger and Goldings whole hops

TASTING NOTES

Nose	Luscious grain and hop aromas
Palate	Full malt body in the mouth with bitter undertones, long dry finish and fruit notes
Comments	A rounded ale with good fruit character, splendid companion for a pub lunch

6   Morrells Brewery Ltd

**Lion Brewery, St Thomas Street, Oxford OX1 1LA
Tel: 0865 792013**

Independent
Reception centre Yes. *Brewery tours* by arrangement

LIGHT ALE

OG 1032° ABV 3.2%
Ingredients: pale malt (87%),
crystal malt (6%), torrefied
wheat (7%). Goldings,
Challenger and Target hop
pellets

TASTING NOTES

Nose	Estery aroma
Palate	Light grain in the mouth, delicate hop notes in finish
Comments	Light quaffing beer

DARK MILD

OG 1033° ABV 3.2%
Ingredients: pale malt (87%), crystal malt (6%),
torrefied wheat (7%). Casks primed with sugar, 6 pints
per barrel. Challenger, Goldings and Target hop
pellets

TASTING NOTES

Nose	Light hints of hop and nut
Palate	Chewy malt in the mouth, short dry finish with roasted notes
Comments	Pleasant malty dark ale

BEST BITTER

OG 1036° ABV 3.7%
Ingredients: pale malt (86%), crystal malt (7%),
torrefied wheat (7%). Goldings, Challenger and
Target hop pellets

TASTING NOTES

Nose	Tempting aromas of hop resin, citric fruit notes
Palate	Delicate balance of grain and hop with light dry finish and faint notes of orange peel
Comments	A carefully balanced copper-coloured beer, brewed for session drinking

VARSITY
OG 1041° ABV 4.3%
Ingredients: pale malt (85%), crystal malt (7%), torrefied wheat (8%). Goldings, Challenger and Target hop pellets

TASTING NOTES

Nose	Powerful wafts of grain and hop with fruit developing
Palate	Full-tasting malt and hop in the mouth, deep bitter-sweet finish with hints of vanilla
Comments	A rich and satisfying ale, good for drinking on its own or through a meal

COLLEGE ALE
OG 1072° ABV 6%
Ingredients: pale malt (89%), crystal malt (6%), torrefied wheat (5%). Goldings, Challenger and Target hop pellets

TASTING NOTES

Nose	Pronounced aromas of roasted grain and rich marmalade fruit
Palate	Heady, sweetish malt and fruit, dense bitter-sweet finish with nuts, raisins and sultanas
Comments	A ripe, golden winter brew "to warm the inner man" says the brewer. It is a "party-gyle" beer with Light Ale, made from the same mash. Celebration Ale (1066) is a bottled beer occasionally sold in draught form

LONDON

For centuries, long before the rise of Burton, London set the pace for the rest of the country and, increasingly, for other parts of the world as well. The brown and dark beers of London and in particular the style known as Entire or Porter were much copied abroad and exported to such unlikely places as the American colonies and Russia. Most of the still famous names in commercial brewing—Whitbread, Truman, Charrington and Courage, for example—sprang to fame and fortune in London. Now only Watney has a brewery in the capital and the Mortlake factory produces just lager and keg beers. Others have moved to "green field" sites alongside motorways as part of the modern trend towards centralised mega breweries. The flag is kept flying by two doughty independents, Fuller and Young, with more recent support from the enthusiasts at the Pitfield micro brewery. Fuller and Young have maintained the heritage of the deeply complex bitter beers that replaced Porter. Their bitters have a pronounced hop character that stresses both London's proximity to the hop fields of Kent and the preference of past generations of working class Londoners who earned money by picking hops and who liked the bite and edge which the plant gave to their ale. The only remaining "big name" left in London is that of Guinness, still concentrating with its Extra Stout on the beer style which transformed the drinking habits of the Irish.

Greater London
Park Royal **2**   **3** Hoxton
Chiswick **1**
4 Wandsworth

Fuller Smith & Turner PLC

**Griffin Brewery, Chiswick Lane South, W4 2QB
Tel: 01-994 3691**

Independent
Reception centre Yes. *Brewery tours* by arrangement

CHISWICK BITTER

OG 1034° ABV 3.5%
Ingredients: pale malt,
crystal malt, flaked
maize, caramel for
colour. Target,
Northdown, Challenger
and Goldings whole and
pellet hops

TASTING NOTES

Nose	Luscious hop resin and light fruit
Palate	Cleansing and quenching balance of malt and hop, light finish with delicate fruit notes
Comments	Superbly quaffable light bitter, Champion Beer of Britain for 1989

LONDON PRIDE

OG 1040° ABV 4.1%
Ingredients: pale malt, crystal malt, flaked maize,
caramel for colour. Target, Northdown and
Challenger hop pellets

TASTING NOTES

Nose	Ripe, developing aromas of grain, hop and fruit
Palate	A multi-layered delight of malt and hops and a deep, intense finish with hop and ripening fruit notes

Comments	An astonishingly complex beer for its gravity, fine for drinking on its own or with well-flavoured food

ESB (EXTRA SPECIAL BITTER)

OG 1054° ABV 5.5%
Ingredients: pale malt, crystal malt, flaked maize, caramel for colour. Target, Northdown, Challenger and Goldings whole and pellet hops

TASTING NOTES

Nose	An explosion of grain, hops and Cooper's marmalade
Palate	Enormous attack of malt and fruit with hop underlay; profound finish with strong Goldings character and hints of orange, lemon, gooseberry and some tannin
Comments	A beer for a Bacchanalia, "perilously drinkable" according to Michael Jackson. It has a cupboardful of medals and other awards

2 Arthur Guinness, Son and Co (Great Britain)

Park Royal Brewery, NW10 7RR
Tel: 01-965 7700

Division of Guinness Brewing Worldwide Ltd
Reception centre Yes. *Brewery tours* by arrangement

GUINNESS EXTRA

(bottle-conditioned)
OG 1040° ABV 4.3%
Ingredients: pale malt, flaked
barley, roasted barley. English
and American whole hops

TASTING NOTES

Nose	Zesty prickle of hops with pronounced roast barley notes
Palate	Ripe bitter-sweet balance with tart fruit and great length of hop, fruit, coffee and chocolate notes
Comments	A world classic, a jet-black beer of enormous complexity and character. The bottle conditioned version is available only in pubs in England and Wales; all other versions, including those in Scottish bars, are filtered and pasteurised.

3   Pitfield Brewery

8 Pitfield Street, N1 6HA
Tel: 01-739 3701

Independent
Reception centre Yes (Ship and Blue Ball, Bundry Street, E2). *Brewery tours* by arrangement

PITFIELD BITTER
OG 1038° ABV 3.7%
Ingredients: pale malt (90%), crystal malt (7%), wheat malt (3%). Goldings whole hops

TASTING NOTES

Nose	Rich grain and hint of Stilton
Palate	Pleasing malt in the mouth, light, hoppy finish
Comment	Excellent, quaffable copper-coloured bitter

DARK STAR
OG 1048° ABV 4.75%
Ingredients: pale malt, crystal malt, wheat malt, roasted barley for colour. Goldings whole hops.

TASTING NOTES

Nose	Blackcurrant and chocolate aromas
Palate	Ripe malt, coffee and fruit in the mouth, intense tannic finish
Comments	A succulent, sipping, tawny brew, judged Champion Beer of Britain in 1987

HOXTON BEST BITTER
OG 1048° ABV 4.75%
Ingredients: pale malt, crystal malt, wheat malt.
Goldings whole hops

TASTING NOTES

Nose	Fragrant grain and orange peel aromas
Palate	Fat malt in the mouth, deep bitter-sweet finish
Comments	Ripe, rounded and complex ruby ale

LONDON PORTER
OG 1058° ABV 5.5%
Ingredients: pale malt, crystal malt, black malt.
Goldings whole hops

TASTING NOTES

Nose	Biscuity roast barley aroma
Palate	Tart balance of grain, dark chocolate and hop, deep finish with leather, coffee and gooseberry notes
Comments	Dark stout of great depth and roastiness, based on a Whitbread recipe of 1850

4   Young & Co PLC

**Ram Brewery, High Street, Wandsworth SW18 4JD
Tel: 01-870 0141**

Independent
Reception centre Yes. *Brewery tours* Yes

BITTER

OG 1036° ABV 3.5%
Ingredients: Maris Otter
pale malt (93%),
torrefied wheat (3%).
Fuggles and Goldings
whole hops

TASTING NOTES

Nose	Lilting aromas of Goldings and malt, delicate citric notes
Palate	Superb tart balance of grain and hop, intense finish with orange and lemon notes
Comments	A real Bow Bells beer with a stunning hoppy edge, ideal as a session beer or with cockles and other fresh sea food. In Young's pubs it is always known as "a pint of Ordinary"

SPECIAL BITTER

OG 1046° ABV 4.5%
Ingredients: Maris Otter pale malt (93%), torrefied wheat (3%). Fuggles and Goldings whole hops

TASTING NOTES

Nose	Ripe grain and hop aromas with orange peel developing
Palate	Rounded malt with good hop underpinning, deep finish with citrous fruit and slight grape notes
Comments	Beautifully crafted and drinkable bitter, exceptionally dry for its gravity

WINTER WARMER

OG 1055° ABV 5.2%
Ingredients: Maris Otter pale malt, crystal malt,
torrefied wheat. Fuggles and Goldings whole hops

TASTING NOTES

Nose	Warm biscuity aromas with vinous notes
Palate	Generous malt and hop with rich port-wine finish
Comments	Ruby old ale brewed for the winter months, superb with blue cheese or nuts

SOUTH-EAST ENGLAND

Hops are grown in other regions, Worcestershire in particular, but Kent is fondly regarded as the hop garden of England. Travellers to and from the Kentish ports have for centuries seen the landscape criss-crossed by tall wired frames that encourage the hop bines to climb towards the sun and the rain. And in between the hop fields there are the strangely cowled oast houses in which the hops are dried and cured after picking. The bucolic picture is tinged with nostalgia, for the Kent hop industry is in sad decline and too many oast houses have been turned into weekend cottages. The rise of Euro-lager and the importing of cheap hops from as far afield as Yugoslavia and even China have led to a sharp—some say terminal decline—in demand for English hops. But as this book makes clear there is still a powerful attachment to traditional English varieties for cask beer production. It is not surprising that many of the ales of South-east England, brewed in the heart of the hop producing area, have a tang and a bite that lingers tartly and refreshingly on the palate.

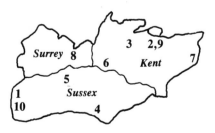

1 Ballard's Brewery Ltd

**Unit C, The Old Sawmill, Nyewood, Rogate,
Petersfield, Hants GU31 5HA Tel: 073 080 362**

Independent
Reception centre No. *Brewery tours* Yes

BEST BITTER

OG 1042° ABV 4.1%
Ingredients: pale malt
(90%), crystal malt
(10%). Fuggles and
Goldings whole hops

TASTING NOTES

Nose	Pleasing aromas of hop resin with fruit developing
Palate	Full mouth filling grain with fine hop balance, long finish with delightful nutty notes
Comments	Excellent refreshing ale, a superb companion for cheese or fish dishes

WASSAIL

OG 1060° ABV 5.7%
Ingredients: pale malt (85%), crystal malt (15%).
Fuggles and Goldings whole hops

TASTING NOTES

Nose	Lovely eddying wafts of grain and ripe fruit
Palate	Fat grain and ripe fruit in mouth, deep finish with complex hop bitterness, sultanas and raisins
Comments	Dark, rich bitter-sweet beer, good with dark meats or blue cheese

2   **Fremlins Ltd**

Court Street, Faversham, Kent   Tel: 0795 533311

Subsidiary of Whitbread
Reception centre Yes. *Brewery tours* by arrangement

FREMLINS BITTER

OG 1035° ABV 3.5%
Ingredients: pale
malt (70%), crystal
malt (4%), torrefied
wheat (12%), sugar
(14%). Hop extract
(100%), dry hopped
with Styrian pellets

TASTING NOTES

Nose	Plenty of hop resin aroma with subtle spiciness
Palate	Light, quenching balance of grain and hop, delicate nutty finish
Comments	Pleasant chestnut-coloured session bitter

POMPEY ROYAL

OG 1043° ABV 4.5%
Ingredients: pale malt (67.5%), crystal malt (7.5%),
torrefied wheat (12.5%), sugar (12.5%). Hop extract
with some Styrian pellets. Dry hopped with Styrians

TASTING NOTES

Nose	Tempting hop and light fruit aromas
Palate	Warm malt in the mouth, long finish with hop and vanilla notes
Comments	Smooth, mahogany coloured ale brewed for the Wessex region: the beer originates from Portsmouth. A cask version of Whitbread Best Bitter was due to be brewed at Faversham in the autumn of 1989

3   Goacher's

**P & D.J Goacher, 5 Hayle Mill Cottages,
Bockingford, Maidstone, Kent ME15 6DT
Tel: 0622 682112**

Independent
Reception centre No. *Brewery tours* Yes

LIGHT MAIDSTONE ALE

OG 1036°
Ingredients: 100% Munton &
Fison pale and crystal malt.
Mid-Kent Goldings and Progress
whole hops

TASTING NOTES

Nose	Intense hop aroma with delicate citric fruit notes
Palate	Mellow balance of hop and grain in mouth, quenching finish
Comments	A superb, pale coloured bitter, a fine Kentish ale, filtered over additional hops in the hop back

DARK MAIDSTONE ALE

OG 1040°
Ingredients: 100% Munton & Fison pale, crystal,
black and chocolate malt. East Kent Goldings and
Progress whole hops

TASTING NOTES

Nose	Complex aromas of roasted malt, coffee and tart fruit
Palate	Deep chewy grain in the mouth, long dry finish with hop and dark chocolate notes
Comments	Deep copper coloured beer, a rare and potable ale

OLD MAIDSTONE ALE

OG 1066°
Ingredients: 100% Munton & Fison pale malt, crystal, black and chocolate malt. East Kent Goldings

TASTING NOTES

Nose	Meaty, toffee, Ribena aromas
Palate	Shockingly dry grain and tart fruit in the mouth, intense finish with hops, raisins and sultana
Comments	A powerful dark winter brew full of intriguing, complex tannic flavours, conditioned in cask in the brewery for three months. Occasional numbered version conditioned in the bottle

4 Harvey & Son (Lewes) Ltd

Bridge Wharf Brewery, 6 Cliffe High Street, Lewes, E Sussex BN7 2AH Tel: 0273 480209

Independent
Reception centre Yes (in brewery shop). *Brewery tours* Yes (12 months' waiting list)

MILD or XX
OG 1030° ABV 3%
Ingredients: mild ale malt and crystal malt, black and caramel sugars. Bramling Cross, Fuggles and Goldings whole hops, most locally grown

TASTING NOTES

Nose	Light nutty grain aroma
Palate	Soft, sweet malt with short finish and delicate hop notes
Comments	Easy drinking, pleasant dark mild

SUSSEX BITTER (PA or Pale Ale)
OG 1033° ABV 3.5%
Ingredients: pale and crystal malt, flaked maize and sugars. Bramling Cross, Fuggles, Goldings and Progress whole hops, most locally grown

TASTING NOTES

Nose	Sweet malt offset by delicate hop aroma
Palate	Good cleansing balance of grain and hop with dry finish
Comments	Light and quenching session bitter

SUSSEX BEST BITTER (BB)

OG 1040° ABV 4%
Ingredients: pale and crystal malt, flaked maize and
sugars. Bramling Cross, Fuggles, Goldings and
Progress whole hops, most locally grown

TASTING NOTES

Nose	Tempting bouquet of rich malt and tangy hop
Palate	Rounded balance of grain and hop with deep dry finish and fruit notes
Comments	Fine bitter-sweet bitter, good with well-flavoured cheese

SUSSEX OLD (XXXX)

OG 1043° ABV 4.2%
Ingredients: mild ale and crystal malt, black and
caramel sugars. Bramling Cross, Fuggles and Goldings
whole hops, most grown locally

TASTING NOTES

Nose	Soft aromas of malt, dried fruit and coffee
Palate	Mellow malt and fruit in the mouth, deep finish with good hop sparkle and complex fruit notes
Comments	Dark, soft and warming winter brew; Harvey's beers are also sold under the name of Beard's, a pub-owning company that no longer brews

5 King & Barnes Ltd

**The Bishopric, Horsham, West Sussex RH12 1QP
Tel: 0403 69341**

Independent
Reception centre Yes. *Brewery tours* Yes (mornings
only)

SUSSEX MILD
OG 1032° ABV 3.4%
Ingredients: pale, crystal
and enzymic malt, maize,
caramel for colour.
Challenger, Goldings,
Worcester Goldings
Variety whole hops

TASTING NOTES

Nose	Delightful light hop and nut aromas
Palate	Sweet malt in the mouth, dry nutty finish
Comments	Good drinking ruby ale

SUSSEX BITTER
OG 1034° ABV 3.6%
Ingredients: pale, crystal and enzymic malt, maize and
caramel. Challenger, Goldings and Worcester
Goldings Variety whole hops

TASTING NOTES

Nose	Rich vanilla and fresh cut grass aromas
Palate	Delicate malt and hop in the mouth, fragrant hop flower finish
Comments	Superb refreshing light bitter

OLD ALE
OG 1045° ABV 4%
Ingredients: pale and crystal malt, torrefied barley,
caramel for colour. Challenger and Worcester
Goldings Variety whole hops

TASTING NOTES

Nose	Fat grain aroma with fruit notes developing
Palate	Full malt and fruit in the mouth, rich hop-and-nut finish
Comments	Round, warming, dark winter brew

FESTIVE

OG 1050° ABV 5%
Ingredients: pale, crystal and enzymic malt, maize, caramel for colour. Challenger and Worcester Goldings Variety whole hops

TASTING NOTES

Nose	Inviting Goldings hop aroma with fruit notes developing
Palate	Mouth-filling sweet grain with good hop balance, deep finish with banana and dried fruit notes
Comments	Powerful dark copper ale with complex balance of flavours

6 **Larkins Brewery Ltd**

**Chiddingstone, Eden Bridge, Kent TN8 7BB
Tel: 0892 49919/870328**

Independent
Reception centre No. *Brewery tours* Yes

TRADITIONAL ALE

OG 1035°
Ingredients: 100% pale
and crystal malt. Fuggles
and East Kent Goldings
whole hops

TASTING NOTES

Nose	Tempting aroma of Goldings
Palate	Light, delicate grain and hop in mouth, quenching finish
Comments	Delectable golden refreshing ale

SOVEREIGN BITTER

OG 1040°
Ingredients: 100% pale and crystal malt. Fuggles and
East Kent Goldings whole hops

TASTING NOTES

Nose	Powerful smack of fresh hops, citric fruit developing
Palate	Rich malt in the mouth with good hop balance, deep dry finish with fruit notes
Comments	Luscious ale, superb on its own or with fish or shell fish

BEST BITTER

OG 1045°
Ingredients: 100% pale and crystal malt. Fuggles and
East Kent Goldings whole hops

TASTING NOTES

Nose	Pronounced grain, hop flower and ripe fruit
Palate	Ripe grain and tart fruit in the mouth, intense finish full of hop and fruit character
Comments	A tasty strong ale with fine malt aroma and taste

PORTER

OG 1053°
Ingredients: 100% pale, crystal and chocolate malt.
Fuggles and East Kent Goldings whole hops

TASTING NOTES

Nose	Strong hop aroma with dark chocolate notes
Palate	Bitter-sweet balance of grain and hop in the mouth, deep fruit and chocolate finish
Comments	A stunning dark, complex winter brew, excellent with walnuts or blue cheese. East Kent Goldings used in all Larkins brews are grown and dried on their own hop farm

7   Martin Ales

Marston Hall, Martin, near Dover, Kent
Tel: 0304 852488

Independent
Reception centre No. *Brewery tours* by arrangement

JOHNSON'S BITTER
OG 1042°

Ingredients: pale malt, wheat malt, crystal malt, flaked
barley, flaked maize. Northdown and Goldings whole
hops in copper and cask

TASTING NOTES

Nose	Lilting aromas of hops and ripe fruit
Palate	Mouth-filling grain with a dry, nutty finish
Comments	Delicious, smooth, dark red ale, surprisingly quenching for its colour: "Not a knife and fork brew," says owner Merrick Johnson who brews in a restored 18th century brewhouse. He has ceased making College Ale (1080°) because of high duty charges but hopes to produce it again

8   Pilgrim Brewery

West Street, Reigate, Surrey
Tel: 07372 22651

Independent
Reception centre No. *Brewery tours* by arrangement

SURREY BITTER

OG 1038°
Ingredients:
pale malt,
torrefied wheat
(3-4%). East
Kent Goldings
whole hops in
copper and cask

THE PILGRIM BREWERY

Reigate, Surrey.
Established in 1982

TASTING NOTES

Nose	Light, tempting hop flower aroma with delicate citric notes
Palate	Cleansing and luscious hop and grain in mouth, light dry finish with faint lemon notes
Comments	Fine, well-balanced refreshing ale

DARK XXXX

OG 1040°
Ingredients: pale malt, torrefied wheat (3-4%), roast malt extract. East Kent whole Goldings hops

TASTING NOTES

Nose	Pleasing aromas of hop and toast
Palate	Chewy grain and dark chocolate in mouth, intense dry finish with coffee notes
Comments	Good tasting strong dark mild

PROGRESS

OG 1041°
Ingredients: pale malt, torrefied wheat (3-4%). East
Kent Goldings whole hops

TASTING NOTES

Nose	Ripe grain and fruit with hop notes
Palate	Full malt in the mouth, deep, rounded bitter-sweet finish with hop and fruit
Comments	Rich tasting ale, good with a ploughman's lunch

TALISMAN

OG 1048°
Ingredients: pale malt, crystal malt, torrefied wheat
(3-4%), invert sugar. East Kent Goldings whole hops

TASTING NOTES

Nose	Deep complex aromas of hop, fruit and tannin
Palate	Superb mouth-feel of malt and tart fruit, deep, polished finish with hop, vanilla and banana notes
Comments	Distinguished strong ale, brewed usually in the winter only

9 Shepherd Neame

**17 Court Street, Faversham, Kent ME13 7AX
Tel: 0795 532206**

Independent
Reception centre Yes. *Brewery tours* Yes

MASTER BREW BITTER

OG 1036° ABV 3.8%
Ingredients: pale malt (75%),
crystal malt (8%), amber malt
(5%), wheat malt (4%),
torrefied wheat (8%) and
glucose syrup. East Kent
Omega, Target and Zenith hop
pellets with Goldings hop oil

TASTING NOTES

Nose	Powerful smack of hop resin
Palate	Dry grainy mouth-feel with long finish full of hop character and light fruit
Comments	A stunning beer from the hop fields

MASTER BREW BEST BITTER

OG 1039° ABV 4%
Ingredients: pale malt (75%), crystal malt (8%),
amber malt (5%), wheat malt (4%), torrefied wheat
(8%) and glucose syrup. East Kent Omega, Target and
Zenith hop pellets with Golding hop oil

TASTING NOTES

Nose	Tart wafts of hop with tangy fruit developing
Palate	Good balance of malt and fruit in the mouth, intense dry finish with citric fruit notes
Comments	Big, bold beer full of delectable hop character; Stock Ale is a winter version with additional colour

10   Sussex Brewery

36 Main Road, Hermitage, Emsworth, W Sussex PO10 8AU Tel: 0243 371533

Independent
Reception centre No. *Brewery tours* Yes (small groups only)

WYNDHAM BITTER

OG 1037°
Ingredients: pale malt (48 kilos per barrel) and crystal malt (2.5 kpb). Challenger and Goldings whole hops

TASTING NOTES

Nose	Strong hop aroma
Palate	Cleansing balance of malt and hop in the mouth, dry finish with good hop character
Comments	Good tasting refreshing light bitter

HERMITAGE BEST BITTER

OG 1047°
Ingredients: pale malt (50 kpb) and crystal malt (3 kpb). Challenger and Goldings whole hops

TASTING NOTES

Nose	Ripe fruity aroma
Palate	Full malt in the mouth, deep finish with good bitter-sweet balance and fruit notes
Comments	Strong amber ale with pleasing, not cloying fruity sweetness

WARRIOR ALE
OG 1057°
Ingredients: pale malt (52 kpb) and crystal malt (4 kpb). Challenger and Goldings whole hops

TASTING NOTES

Nose	Scintillating floral hop bouquet with fat fruit notes
Palate	Big malt in the mouth, long, dry finish with powerful hop character and ripe fruit
Comments	Rich and tasty strong ale; Sussex also brews a summer-only Sussex Pale Ale (1034°) and a Lumley Old Ale (1056°) for the winter: not tasted

SOUTH-WEST ENGLAND

Thomas Hardy's love of good country ale was
repaid by the Dorchester brewers Eldridge Pope,
whose Thomas Hardy's Ale includes on its label a
quotation from *The Trumpet Major* extolling the
virtues of the beer of "Casterbridge". The present
day beers of Wessex have noticeably full and rather
dry palates, tending towards a fruity astringency in
Gale's ales and to a delectable hint of nut in
Palmer's and Hall & Woodhouse's products.
Further north, Whitbread's Cheltenham brewery
supplies much of the group's cask beer
requirements. Once proud and independent
brewers such as Flowers of Stratford, Strong of
Romsey and Wethered of Marlow have been closed
with an attempt to replicate their fine brews under
one roof. The new Cheltenham version of
Wethered's Bitter shows that it is always preferable
to leave well alone. In the Cotswolds, Claude
Arkell's Donnington company reaffirms one's faith
in small craft breweries, delectable ale produced in
serene surroundings and sold in fine old stone pubs.

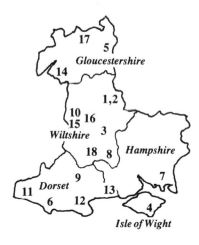

1   Archers Ales Ltd

London Street, Swindon, Wilts SN1 5DG
Tel: 0793 496789

Independent
Reception centre Yes ("sort of"). *Brewery tours* Yes:
trade and CAMRA groups only

VILLAGE BITTER

OG 1035° ABV 3.2%
Ingredients: pale malt (95%),
crystal malt (5%). Sunshine
and Fuggles whole hops, late
hopped (i.e. towards the end
of the boil) with East Kent
Goldings pellets

TASTING NOTES

Nose	Light hop aroma
Palate	Delicate balance of grain and hop, cleansing finish
Comments	Good refreshing session bitter

BEST BITTER

OG 1040° ABV 4.1%
Ingredients: pale malt (95%), crystal malt (5%).
Sunshine and Fuggles whole hops, late hopped with
East Kent Goldings pellets

TASTING NOTES

Nose	Powerful smack of hops and spices
Palate	Tart and tangy grain and hop in the mouth, dry, quenching finish with some citric notes
Comments	An uncompromisingly hoppy beer, a fine thirst-quencher or companion for ripe cheese

ASB

OG 1048° ABV 4.7%
Ingredients: pale malt (95%), crystal malt (5%).
Sunshine and Fuggles whole hops, late hopped with
East Kent Goldings pellets

TASTING NOTES

Nose	Great wafts of Goldings aroma with tart fruit notes
Palate	Fat malt in the mouth with hop edge, deep, intense finish with strong hop character and ripe fruit
Comments	Luscious strong ale, fine for drinking through a meal

HEADBANGER

OG 1065° ABV 6.5%
Ingredients: pale malt (95%), crystal malt (5%).
Sunshine and Fuggles whole hops, late hopped with
East Kent Goldings pellets

TASTING NOTES

Nose	Massive hop and marmalade fruit
Palate	Rich and complex flavours merging into a long finish full of hop, banana, sultana and other fruit notes
Comments	A ripe and complex strong ale, sipped with caution and appreciation. Archers have introduced a Porter (1045°) and also brew an occasional Golden Bitter (1053°); not tasted

2   J Arkell & Sons Ltd

Kingsdown Brewery, Upper Stratton, Swindon, Wilts SN2 6RU Tel: 0793 82 3026

Independent
Reception centre Yes. *Brewery tours* by arrangement

JOHN ARKELL BITTER (BB)

OG 1032° ABV 3.2%
Ingredients: pale malt (90%), crystal malt (6%), sugar (4%). Fuggles, Goldings and Progress whole hops

TASTING NOTES

Nose	Light aromatic hop aroma
Palate	Quenching, slightly tart with dry hop finish
Comments	Fine quaffable session bitter

ARKELL BEST BITTER (3Bs)

OG 1038° ABV 3.6%
Ingredients: pale malt (88%), roasted barley (10%), sugar (2%). Fuggles, Goldings and Progress whole hops

TASTING NOTES

Nose	Powerful aromas of hop flowers and grain
Palate	Delicate, beautifully balanced malt and hop with lingering dry finish and hint of nut
Comments	A superb, memorable amber beer

KINGSDOWN ALE

OG 1052° ABV 5%
Ingredients: pale malt (86%), roasted barley (12%),
sugar (2%). Fuggles, Goldings and Progress whole
hops

TASTING NOTES

Nose	Rich aromas of hop and ripe fruit
Palate	Fat grain and fruit in the mouth, deep bitter-sweet finish with fruit notes. Kingsdown Ale is brewed as a "party-gyle" beer with Best Bitter, that is both from the same mash

3   Bunces Brewery

The Old Mill, Mill Road, Netheravon, Wilts SP4 9QB Tel: 0980 70631

Independent
Reception centre No. *Brewery tours* Yes

BENCHMARK
OG 1033° ABV 3%
Ingredients: Maris Otter pale
malt (84%), crystal malt
(7.5%), wheat flour (8.5%).
Challenger and Goldings
whole hops

TASTING NOTES

Nose	Tart, aromatic hop and light fruit
Palate	Good malt feel in the mouth, fresh cleansing finish
Comments	Light refreshing bitter

BEST BITTER
OG 1042° ABV 4%
Ingredients: Maris Otter pale malt (84%), crystal malt
(7.5%), wheat flour (8.5%). Challenger and Goldings
whole hops

TASTING NOTES

Nose	Delicate flowery aroma
Palate	Fruity and slightly acidic leading to dry hoppy finish
Comments	Golden quenching ale

OLD SMOKEY
OG 1050° ABV 4.5%
Ingredients: Maris Otter pale malt (88%), brown malt
(3.5%), wheat flour (8.5%). Challenger and Goldings
whole hops

TASTING NOTES

Nose	Spicy aroma with a hint of wood smoke
Palate	Dry mouth feel with long, rounded bitter-sweet finish
Comments	Rich, slightly sulphury, deep copper ale. Owner Tony Bunce is something of a brewing poet; he describes his beers as having colours like "a touch of evening sun" or in the case of Old Smokey "darkly transparent; glowing embers seen through smoked glass".

4   Burt's Brewery Ltd

119 High Street, Ventnor, Isle of Wight
Tel: 0983 852153

Reception centre No. *Brewery tours* Yes

BITTER
1030°
Ingredients: pale
ale malt. Fuggles,
Goldings and
Northern Brewer
whole hops

TASTING NOTES

Nose	Delicate hop aroma
Palate	Light malt in the mouth, pleasant bitter-sweet finish
Comments	Easy-going light session bitter; Mild is the same beer with caramel

VPA (VENTNOR PALE ALE)
OG 1040°
Ingredients: pale ale malt. Fuggles, Goldings and
Northern Brewer whole hops

TASTING NOTES

Nose	Ripe bouquet of hop with fruit notes
Palate	Big malt in the mouth, overlaid by good hop balance, deep dry finish with light fruit
Comments	Superb, characterful bitter, Burt's flagship brew; 4X in winter is VPA with added colour

5 Donnington Brewery

**Stow-on-the-Wold, Cheltenham, Glos GL54 1EP
Tel: 0451 30603**

Independent
Reception centre No. *Brewery tours* No

XXX

OG 1035°
Ingredients: Maris Otter
pale malt (85%), invert
sugar (10%), caramel
(5%). Goldings pellet
hops

TASTING NOTES

Nose	Light, delicate hop aroma
Palate	Sweet grain in the mouth with hints of fruit, chocolate and liquorice in the finish
Comments	A delectable dark beer, available in only a few outlets

BB

OG 1036°
Ingredients: Maris Otter pale malt (90%), invert sugar (10%). Goldings pellet hops

TASTING NOTES

Nose	Zesty promise of grain and hop
Palate	Finely-tuned nutty balance, long dry finish
Comments	Delightful, quenching, copper-coloured bitter

SBA

OG 1042°
Ingredients: Maris Otter pale malt (90%), invert sugar
(10%). Goldings pellet hops

TASTING NOTES

Nose	Warm tannic aroma with fruit notes developing
Palate	Rich, rounded balance of malt and hop, dry finish with hints of fruit
Comments	Succulent ale, good with ripe cheese

6   Eldridge Pope & Co PLC

**Dorchester Brewery, Dorchester, Dorset DT1 1QT
Tel: 0305 251251**

Independent
Reception centre Yes. *Brewery tours* Yes

DORCHESTER BITTER

OG 1033° ABV 3.3%
Ingredients: Maris Otter pale
malt and crystal malt. English
whole hops, dry hopped with
English Goldings

TASTING NOTES

Nose	Delicate resiny hop aroma
Palate	Light balance of grain and hop with lingering hop finish
Comments	Quaffable amber ale

DORSET ORIGINAL IPA

OG 1040° ABV 4.2%
Ingredients: Maris Otter pale malt and crystal malt.
English whole hops, dry hopped with Styrian Goldings

TASTING NOTES

Nose	Tempting Goldings aroma with fruit notes developing
Palate	Full grain in the mouth developing a long, cleansing tart finish
Comments	Russet ale of great depth

ROYAL OAK

OG 1048° ABV 5%
Ingredients: Maris Otter pale malt, crystal malt.
English whole hops, dry hopped with English Goldings

TASTING NOTES

Nose	Rich promise of hop and fruit
Palate	Mouth-filling malt and fruit with delicate dry, bitter-sweet finish with pronounced pear drops flavour
Comments	Deep amber ale of great complexity and character; superb with all strong flavoured foods

THOMAS HARDY'S ALE

(bottle conditioned)
OG 1125° ABV 12%
Ingredients: Maris Otter pale malt, crystal malt.
English aroma hops

TASTING NOTES

Nose	"Brisk as a volcano"
Palate	"Full in body; piquant, yet without a twang; free from streakiness"
Comments	"Luminous as an autumn sunset...the most beautiful colour that the eye of an artist in beer could desire". Tasting notes courtesy Mr T. Hardy of Casterbridge. Each bottle is individually numbered and the beer will improve with age

7   **George Gale & Co Ltd**

The Brewery, Horndean, Portsmouth, Hants PO8 0DA Tel: 0705 594050

Independent
Reception centre Yes. *Brewery tours* Yes

XXXL MILD

OG 1030° ABV 3%
Ingredients: Maris
Otter pale malt
(82%), sugar (18%),
black malt. Fuggles, Goldings and
Challenger whole and pellet hops

TASTING NOTES

Nose	Delicate hop aroma
Palate	Light grain in the mouth, short finish with some hop notes and faint hints of coffee
Comments	A malty light mild

XXXD MILD

OG 1030° ABV 3%
Ingredients: Maris Otter pale malt (82%), sugar
(18%), black malt and caramel. Fuggles, Goldings and
Challenger whole and pellet hops

TASTING NOTES

Nose	Faint hop aroma and chocolate
Palate	Sweet malt in the mouth, gentle finish with vanilla notes
Comments	Similar to the light mild

BBB or BUTSER BREW BITTER

OG 1036° ABV 3.6%
Ingredients: Maris Otter pale malt (80%), sugar
(18%), torrefied wheat (2%). Fuggles, Goldings and
Challenger whole and pellet hops

TASTING NOTES

Nose	Ripe hop and lemon aromas
Palate	Deep and complex grain and hop in mouth with long, tart finish and slight astringency
Comments	Uncompromising tart, tangy pale bitter

XXXX

OG 1044° ABV 4.2%
Ingredients: Maris Otter pale malt (88%), sugar
(10%), torrefied wheat (2%), black malt and caramel.
Fuggles, Goldings and Challenger whole and pellet hops

TASTING NOTES

Nose	Smokey aroma with hop and fruit hints
Palate	Sweet malt in the mouth, deep, rounded hop and fruit finish
Comments	Dark and warming winter ale

HORNDEAN SPECIAL BITTER

OG 1050° ABV 4.5%
Ingredients: Maris Otter pale malt (80%), sugar
(15%), torrefied wheat (5%), black malt. Fuggles,
Goldings and Challenger whole and pellet hops

TASTING NOTES

Nose	Ripe fruit and hop aromas
Palate	Fat malt with hop edge in the mouth, intense finish with citric and faint chocolate notes
Comments	Complex, slightly sour strong beer, would go well with salty shell fish

PRIZE OLD ALE (bottle conditioned)

OG 1094° ABV 8.5%
Ingredients: Maris Otter pale malt (98%), black malt,
wheat. Fuggles and Goldings whole and pellet hops

TASTING NOTES

Nose	Stunning, complex aromas of hop, ripe fruit including apple notes
Palate	Great mouth-filling malt and fruit in the mouth, intensely dry fruity finish with raisin hints
Comments	Superb deep red barley wine, the only beer in corked bottles

8 Gibbs Mew PLC

Anchor Brewery, Gigant Street, Salisbury, Wilts SP1 2AR Tel: 0722 411911

Independent
Reception centre No. *Brewery tours* by arrangement

WILTSHIRE TRADITIONAL BITTER

OG 1036° ABV 3.5%
Ingredients not revealed

TASTING NOTES

Nose	Fresh hop and grain aromas
Palate	Pleasing balance in the mouth, delicate hop finish
Comments	Light supping bitter

SALISBURY BEST BITTER
OG 1042° ABV 4.2%
Ingredients not revealed

TASTING NOTES

Nose	Malt aromas with pineapple developing
Palate	Sweet grain in mouth, light malty finish with late dryness and dried fruit
Comments	A fruity copper-coloured bitter, excellent with a ploughman's lunch

PREMIUM BITTER
OG 1042° ABV 4.2%
Ingredients not revealed

TASTING NOTES

Nose	Ripe malt with some fruit notes

Palate	Fat grain in the mouth, sweet finish with some fruit notes

Comments	Mellow ale lacking hop character

THE BISHOP'S TIPPLE
OG 1066° ABV 6.5%
Ingredients: pale and crystal malt. Goldings, Fuggles and Challenger hops

TASTING NOTES

Nose	Complex grainy, earthy aromas with hint of toffee
Palate	Great mouth-filling grain and fruit leading into deep vinous finish and chocolate notes
Comments	A barley wine to make you lose your mitre

9 Hall & Woodhouse Ltd

**The Brewery, Blandford Forum, Dorset DT11 9LS
Tel: 0258 52141**

Independent
Reception centre Yes. *Brewery tours* Yes

BADGER BEST BITTER

OG 1040° ABV 4%
Ingredients: pale malt,
crystal malt, caramel,
copper sugars.
Challenger, Northdown
and Worcester Goldings
Variety hop pellets

TASTING NOTES

Nose	Pronounced hop and grain aromas, fruit notes developing
Palate	Ripe, rounded balance in mouth leading to dry hop finish with pleasing hints of nut
Comments	Superb copper-coloured ale

TANGLEFOOT

OG 1047° ABV 4.9%
Ingredients: pale malt, copper sugars. Challenger,
Northdown and Worcester Goldings Variety whole
and pellet hops

TASTING NOTES

Nose	Rich hop and citrous aromas
Palate	Mouth-filling hop and malt, lingering finish with hop and fruit notes and slight hints of nut
Comments	A quenching ale, drinks more comfortably than gravity suggests

10   Mole's Brewery

Wayward Ltd, Merlin Way, Bowerhill, Melksham, Wilts SN12 6TJ Tel: 0225 704734

Independent
Reception centre No. *Brewery tours* Yes

MOLE'S CASK BITTER

OG 1040° ABV 3.9%
Ingredients: pale malt
(90%), crystal malt (10%).
Progress and Worcester
Goldings variety whole
hops

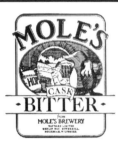

TASTING NOTES

Nose	Grain aromas with subtle hint of hop
Palate	Delicate malt in mouth with lingering hop finish
Comments	Cleansing balance of grain and hop, a refreshing bitter

11   J.C. & R.H. Palmer Ltd

Old Brewery, Bridport, Dorset DT6 4JA Tel: 0308 22396

Independent
Reception centre Yes. *Brewery tours* Yes

BRIDPORT BITTER (BB)

OG 1032° ABV 3.2%
Ingredients: 100% pale malt. Goldings whole hops

TASTING NOTES

Nose	Delicate hints of hop and grain
Palate	Cleansing light balance of malt and hop with dry, slightly nutty finish
Comments	Now rare example of a Dorset "boy's bitter" with a floral quenching palate

IPA
OG 1039° ABV 4.25%
Ingredients: 100% pale malt. Goldings whole hops

TASTING NOTES

Nose	Nostril-quivering aromas of rich hop and grain
Palate	Full malt in the mouth with intense dry attenuated finish and fine balance of hop, fruit and nut
Comments	A delectable beer; in a Guild of Beer Writers' tasting of 10 classic British ales unanimous choice as beer of the show

TALLY HO!
OG 1046° ABV 4.64%
Ingredients: 100% pale malt plus caramel for colour. Goldings whole hops

TASTING NOTES

Nose	Pronounced hop and nut aromas
Palate	Rich, sweet malt in the mouth, long finish with complex balance of fruit, hop and nut
Comments	A dark strong ale, fine with well-flavoured food. Head brewer Peter Seed is a full malt mash man: "I don't use anything else; I won't mess around with maize or torrefied wheat."

12   Poole Brewery

**38 Sandbanks Road, Poole, Dorset BH15 1DA
Tel: 0202 682345**

Independent
Reception centre Yes (Brewhouse pub, High St).
Brewery tours by arrangement

POOLE BEST BITTER
or DOLPHIN BITTER

OG 1039° ABV 4.2%
Ingredients: pale malt
(87.5%), crystal malt
(12.5%), cane sugar,
caramel for colour. Kent
Goldings (30%+10%
after boil), Worcester Fuggles
(50%), Goldings dry hopped (10%).

(logo: POOLE · BREWERY)

TASTING NOTES

Nose	Lilt of fresh hops
Palate	Fine balance of malt and hops in mouth, lingering finish with hop and nut flavours
Comments	A deep amber refreshing ale

BOSUN BEST BITTER

OG 1049° ABV 5.5%
Ingredients: pale malt (85%), crystal malt (15%),
roasted barley and chocolate malt for colour, cane
sugar syrup. 100% Kent whole Goldings hops

TASTING NOTES

Nose	Booming Goldings aroma
Palate	Mellow malt in the mouth, dry hoppy finish
Comments	A rich, amber ale. The beers are kept under carbon dioxide pressure in the company's Brewhouse pub; 20 free trade outlets

13 Ringwood Brewery

**Christchurch Road, Ringwood, Hants BH24 3AP
Tel: 0425 471177**

Independent
Reception centre No. *Brewery tours* Yes (winter only)

BEST BITTER

OG 1038° ABV 3.7%
Ingredients: Maris
Otter pale malt
(94%), wheat flour.
Goldings and
Worcester Goldings
Variety hop pellets

TASTING NOTES

Nose	Tempting hop resin aroma with light fruit notes
Palate	Good malt feel in the mouth, dry, tangy, fruit finish
Comments	Delicious, easy-drinking slightly tart pale bitter

FORTYNINER

OG 1048° ABV 4.7%
Ingredients: Maris Otter pale malt (94%), wheat flour.
Goldings and Worcester Goldings Variety hop pellets

TASTING NOTES

Nose	Light, fresh hop bouquet
Palate	Rounded malt in the mouth with strong hop balance, deep bitter-sweet finish with delicate fruit notes

XXXX PORTER

OG 1048° ABV 4.2%
Ingredients: Maris Otter pale malt and crystal malt
(92%), wheat flour, chocolate malt and caramel.
Goldings and Worcester Variety Goldings hop pellets

TASTING NOTES

Nose	Rich aromas of hop and toast
Palate	Dry in the mouth with burnt malt notes, dry nutty finish
Comments	Smooth drinking dark beer with delectable chewy grain feel

OLD THUMPER

OG 1058° ABV 5.7%
Ingredients: Maris Otter pale malt (92%), wheat flour.
Goldings and Worcester Goldings Variety hop pellets

TASTING NOTES

Nose	Peppery, spicy aroma with hint of apple and nettles
Palate	Luscious balance of grain and hop in the mouth, bitter- sweet finish with good hop tingle and citric notes
Comments	Warm, rounded yet surprisingly delicate pale strong beer; voted Champion Beer of Britain in 1988

14 Uley Brewery Ltd

**The Old Brewery, Uley, Dursley, Glos GL11 5TB
Tel: 0453 860120**

Independent
Reception centre No. *Brewery tours* by arrangement

HOGSHEAD

OG 1037°
Ingredients: pale Devonshire
malt, crystal malt.
Worcestershire Fuggles and
Goldings whole hops

TASTING NOTES

Nose	Light hop and grain
Palate	Cleansing balance of malt and hop, tangy finish
Comments	Refreshing session bitter

ULEY BITTER

OG 1040°
Ingredients: pale Devonshire malt, crystal malt.
Worcestershire Fuggles and Goldings whole hops

TASTING NOTES

Nose	Ripe malt and hop aromas, fruit developing
Palate	Fat malt in the mouth, deep dry finish with pronounced Lemon notes
Comments	Superb 5-star bitter

OLD SPOT PRIZE ALE

OG 1050°
Ingredients: pale Devonshire malt (85%), crystal malt
(15%). Worcestershire Fuggles and Goldings whole
hops

███████████████████████████████████████

TASTING NOTES

Nose	Delectable hop resin aroma with ripe fruit developing
Palate	Rich, rounded malt in the mouth, long bitter-sweet finish with tart fruitiness
Comments	Superbly balanced strong ale, accounts for 75% of production

PIG'S EAR

OG 1050°
Ingredients: lager malt (100%). Worcestershire
Fuggles and Goldings whole hops

TASTING NOTES

Nose	Rich butterscotch and lemon aromas
Palate	Stunning balance of light malt and hop bitterness, deep finish with hop flower and citrous notes
Comments	A hybrid of lager malt and English hops, a pale, deceptively strong beer, brewed to wean young drinkers off Euro-lager. Uley has also introduced a winter beer called Pigor Mortis (sic) 1058°, 80% pale malt, 20% crystal; not tasted

5 Ushers Brewery Ltd

Parade House, Fore Street, Trowbridge, Wilts BA14 8JY Tel: 0225 763171

Susidiary of Grand Metropolitan Brewing
Reception centre Yes. *Brewery tours* by arrangement

USHERS BEST BITTER

OG 1038° ABV 3.4%
Ingredients: Maris Otter or
Triumph pale malt (81%), crystal
malt (4%), syrup (15%). Various
hop pellets, late copper Goldings

TASTING NOTES

Nose	Good hop and spice aromas
Palate	Sweetish malt in the mouth, dry finish with toffee notes
Comments	Pleasant bitter. Ushers are now brewing Truman Best Bitter (OG 1044°) since the closure of the London brewery; Wiltshire version not tasted; it is brewed for the London and Essex area

Wadworth & Co Ltd

Northgate Brewery, Devizes, Wilts SN10 1JW Tel: 0380 3361/7

Independent
Reception centre Yes. *Brewery tours* by arrangement

DEVIZES BITTER

OG 1030° ABV 3.2%
Ingredients: Triumph pale
malt (89%), crystal malt
(3%), sugar (8%), caramel
for colour adjustment.
Fuggles whole hops in the
copper, Goldings pellets for dry hopping

TASTING NOTES

Nose	Light grain and hop aromas
Palate	Gentle malt in the mouth, light dry, nutty finish
Comments	Tasty light "boy's bitter"

HENRY WADWORTH IPA

OG 1035° ABV 3.8%
Ingredients: Triumph pale malt (89%), crystal malt
(3%), sugar (8%), caramel for colour adjustment.
Fuggles whole hops in the copper, Goldings pellets for
dry hopping

TASTING NOTES

Nose	Good hop aroma and light fruit
Palate	Fine malt in the mouth, dry hoppy finish
Comments	A well-attenuated bitter

6X

OG 1040° ABV 4.3%
Ingredients: Triumph pale malt (89%), crystal malt
(3%), sugar (8%), caramel for colour adjustment.
Fuggles whole hops in the copper, Goldings pellets for
dry hopping

TASTING NOTES

Nose	Earthy hop, fruit and nutty grain aromas
Palate	Complex bitter-sweet palate, long dry finish with vanilla notes

Comments	Copper-coloured rounded ale of enormous depth and quality; Wadworth's flagship beer

FARMER'S GLORY

OG 1046° ABV 4.5%
Ingredients: Triumph pale malt (89%), crystal malt (3%), sugar (8%), caramel and roasted malt extract for colour and flavour. Fuggles whole hops in the copper, Goldings pellets for dry hopping

TASTING NOTES

Nose	Rich, delightful aromas of Goldings and toast
Palate	Full grain and hop in the mouth, deep dry finish with roast barley notes
Comments	A ripe and tasty deep red strong ale, excellent with smoked fish or cheese

OLD TIMER

OG 1055° ABV 5.8%
Ingredients: Triumph pale malt (89%), crystal malt (3%), sugar (8%), caramel for colour adjustment. Fuggles whole hops in the copper, Goldings pellets for dry hopping

TASTING NOTES

Nose	Ripe fruit and hop aromas
Palate	Fat grain and fruit in the mouth, intense finish full of hop bitterness with banana and sultana notes
Comments	Heavy, aromatic winter beer: "ideal by a log fire" says the head brewer

17 **Whitbread (Cheltenham)**

Monson Avenue, Cheltenham, Glos
Tel: 0242 521401

Subsidiary of Whitbread
Reception centre Yes. *Brewery tours* by arrangement

WEST COUNTRY PALE ALE
OG 1030° ABV 3.1%
Ingredients: pale malt (65%), crystal malt (7.5%),
torrefied wheat (15%), sugar (12.5%). 90% hop
extract, 10% Target pellets. Dry hopped with Target

TASTING NOTES

Nose	Light hop aroma
Palate	Light, refreshing malt and hop balance, delicate hoppy finish
Comments	Quenching light session beer, good example of a "boy's bitter"

WETHEREDS BITTER
OG 1035° ABV 3.6%
Ingredients: pale malt (65%), crystal malt (7.5%),
torrefied wheat (15%), sugar (12.5%). 90% hop
extract, 10% Target pellets. Dry hopped with Target

TASTING NOTES

Nose	Grain and tangerine aromas
Palate	Light hop and grain in mouth, dry, tangy finish with some astringency
Comments	A dry amber beer that has lost its typical Marlow estery character since "going west"

FLOWERS IPA
OG 1036° ABV 3.6%
Ingredients: pale malt (65%), crystal malt (7.5%),
torrefied wheat (15%), sugar (12.5%). 90% hop
extract, 10% target pellets. Dry hopped with Target

TASTING NOTES

Nose	Light hop aroma with hint of apple
Palate	Good balance of grain and hop in the mouth, light bitter-sweet finish
Comments	Easy drinking light bitter

STRONG COUNTRY BITTER

OG 1037° ABV 3.9%
Ingredients: pale malt (65%), crystal malt (7.5%),
torrefied wheat (15%), sugar (12.5%). 90% hop
extract, 10% Target pellets. Dry hopped with Target

TASTING NOTES

Nose	Good hop aroma with hint of banana
Palate	Delicate balance of malt and hop, dry and tart finish
Comments	A pale, slightly flinty bitter

WETHERED SPA

OG 1040° ABV 4.2%
Ingredients: pale malt (65%), crystal (7.5%), torrefied
wheat (15%), sugar (12.5%). 90% hop extract, 10%
Target pellets. Dry hopped with Target

TASTING NOTES

Nose	Hop and spice aromas
Palate	Full malt in the mouth with hop edge, long dry finish with hint of orange peel
Comments	Rounded, pleasant bitter but lacking the distinctive Marlow feel; Wethereds Winter Royal (1055° ABV 5.7%) is now brewed at Cheltenham: not tasted

FLOWERS ORIGINAL

OG 1044° ABV 4.5%
Ingredients: pale malt (65%), crystal malt (7.5%),
torrefied wheat (15%), sugar (12.5%). 95% hop
extract, 5% Styrian pellets. Dry hopped with Target
pellets

TASTING NOTES

Nose	Rich bouquet of hop and wholemeal biscuit
Palate	Fat malt in the mouth with hop edge, dry finish with some hop character and raisin and sultana notes
Comments	Strong, fruity bitter with some acidity

8   Wiltshire Brewery Company PLC

Stonehenge Brewery, Church Street, Tisbury, Wilts SP3 6NH Tel: 0747 870666

Independent
Reception centre Yes. *Brewery tours* by arrangement

LOCAL BITTER
OG 1035° ABV 3.5%
Ingredients: pale malt
(92%), crystal malt
(4%), amber malt (4%).
Fuggles and Goldings
whole hops

TASTING NOTES

Nose	Delicate, appetising hop aroma
Palate	Light balance of malt and hop in the mouth with lingering dry finish
Comments	Golden, easy drinking session bitter

STONEHENGE BEST BITTER
OG 1041° ABV 4%
Ingredients: pale malt (90%), crystal malt (5%),
amber malt (5%). Fuggles and Goldings whole hops

TASTING NOTES

Nose	Rich malt and ripe fruit aromas
Palate	Ripe malt and fruit in the mouth, deep finish with hop and fruit character
Comments	Pale, full-flavoured bitter that suggests a stronger gravity

OLDE GRUMBLE
OG 1049° ABV 5%
Ingredients: pale malt (97%), crystal malt (2%), sugar
(1%). Fuggles and Goldings whole hops

TASTING NOTES

Nose	Powerful aroma of hop resins
Palate	Ripe, rounded balance of malt and hop with long hop and fruit finish
Comments	Deceptive golden brew, rich and complex

OLD DEVIL
OG 1059° ABV 6%
Ingredients: pale malt (91%), crystal malt (4%),
amber malt (4%), sugar (1%). Fuggles and Goldings
whole hops

TASTING NOTES

Nose	Enticing hop and spicy fruit aromas
Palate	Rich malt in the mouth offset by good hoppy edge with complex finish of hop, fruit and nut
Comments	A powerful, sipping strong ale. Wiltshire also produces a bottled "real" ginger beer from 100% malt, root ginger and Goldings hops

WEST COUNTRY

The West Country is a remote and idiosyncratic region, dependent on summer visitors for its income and yet remarkably indifferent to them: Devonians refer to tourists by the dismissive nickname of "Grockles" while more radical Cornish people will even lapse into their own dense Celtic tongue when confronted by "vurriners". There is no single, distinctive beer style: the ales of Avon and Somerset have a ripe malty fruitiness while further west there is a sharper, even astringent edge to beers that also enjoy a rounded grain character. Several brewers produce deceptively strong and pale beers. Although it falls outside the scope of this book, beer lovers who visit Cornwall should not miss the singular, heady delights of the renowned home-brew pub in Helston, the Blue Anchor, whose Medium bitter has a gravity of 1050° and whose strongest offering, Extra Special, weighs in at 1070°: scarcely "boy's bitters"!

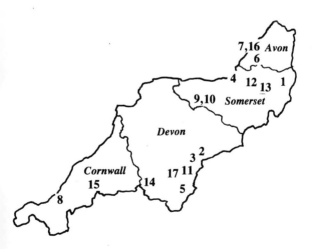

1 Ash Vine Brewery

White Hart, Trudoxhill, Frome, Somerset BA11 5DP Tel: 0373 84324

Independent
Reception centre Yes (White Hart). *Brewery tours* by arrangement

ASH VINE BITTER

OG 1039°
Ingredients: pale malt, crystal malt, wheat flour. Goldings and Worcester Goldings Variety whole hops

TASTING NOTES

Nose	Fresh floral hop aroma with citric notes
Palate	Dry ester and grain in mouth, deep, intensely dry finish
Comments	Good, old-fashioned no-nonsense ale

2   Barron Brewery

**Land Farm, Silverton, nr Exeter, Devon EX5 4HF
Tel: 0392 860406**

Independent
Reception centre No. *Brewery tours* by arrangement

EXE VALLEY BITTER

· OG 1041.5°
Ingredients: pale malt
(95%), roasted barley
(5%). Fuggles whole
hops

TASTING NOTES

Nose	Powerful hop aroma with roasted notes
Palate	Rich mouth-feel of grain and roast barley, long bitter finish with good nut character
Comments	Pale amber beer with pleasing attraction of roast barley; based on old West Country recipe

DEVON GLORY

OG 1049°
Ingredients: pale malt (95%), roasted barley (5%).
Fuggles whole hops

TASTING NOTES

Nose	Rich aromas of grain, roast barley and Fuggles
Palate	Great depth in mouth of sweet grain and chewy roast, long rounded finish with hop, fruit and roast/nut notes
Comments	Rich amber strong ale. The beers are brewed on a farm, using water from their own well

3 Beer Engine

Newton St Cyres, Exeter, Devon EX5 5AX
Tel: 0392 851282

Independent
*Reception centre*s Yes (in pub). *Brewery tours* by
arrangement

RAIL ALE

OG 1037° ABV 4.5%
Ingredients: pale malt
(96%), crystal malt
(4%). Challenger and
Goldings whole hops

TASTING NOTES

Nose	Delicate fresh hop aroma
Palate	Cleasing balance of malt and hop, light dry finish
Comments	Pleasant supping light golden bitter

PISTON BITTER

OG 1044° ABV 5%
Ingredients: pale malt (96.6%), crystal malt (3%),
chocolate malt (1.4%). Challenger and Goldings
whole hops

TASTING NOTES

Nose	Grain and hop aromas

Palate	Good mouth feel of malt, hop and slight chocolate, bitter-sweet finish
Comments	Tasty amber-coloured ale

SLEEPER HEAVY
OG 1055° ABV 6%
Ingredients: pale malt (96.6%), crystal malt (2.4%), chocolate malt (1%). Challenger and Goldings whole hops

TASTING NOTES

Nose	Rich hop resin and coffee aromas
Palate	Full malt and hop in the mouth with deep, intensely dry finish
Comments	Strong dark amber ale with fine balance; the beers are brewed in a pub alongside the Exeter-Barnstaple railway and sold to the free trade

4   Berrow

**Coast Road, Berrow, Burnham-on-Sea, Somerset
Tel: 027 875 345**

Independent
Reception centre No. *Brewery tours* by arrangement

BBBB

OG 1038°
Ingredients: pale malt and
crystal malt. Fuggles and
Goldings hops

TASTING NOTES

Nose	Fine floral aroma with some fruit notes
Palate	Good grain and hop balance in mouth, quenching finish with hop and fruit notes
Comments	Potable amber ale that drinks more than its gravity

TOPSY TURVEY

OG 1055°
Ingredients: 100% pale malt. Fuggles and Goldings
hops

TASTING NOTES

Nose	Powerful aromas of grain and hop with some citric fruit notes
Palate	Fine balance of malt and hop, intense finish of hop bitterness and lemon notes
Comments	A pale, deceptive strong bitter

5   Blackawton Brewery

**Washbourne, Totnes, Devon TQ9 7UF
Tel: 080 423 339**

Independent
Reception centre No. *Brewery tours* No

BLACKAWTON BITTER

OG 1037.5° ABV 3.9%
Ingredients: 100% pale and crystal malt.
Challenger, East Kent Goldings and
Northern Brewer whole hops

TASTING NOTES

Nose	Fresh, floral hop resin aroma
Palate	Good balance of grain and hop with cleansing dry finish
Comments	Refreshing copper-coloured bitter

FORTY FOUR

OG 1044.5° ABV 4.5%
Ingredients: 100% pale and crystal malt. Challenger
and East Kent Goldings whole hops

TASTING NOTES

Nose	Ripe grain and hop with fruit notes developing
Palate	Rounded malt in the mouth, long dry finish with balance of hop bitterness and fruit
Comments	Mellow, smooth-drinking copper ale, good with cheese

HEADSTRONG

OG 1051.5° ABV 5.2%
Ingredients: 100% pale and crystal malt. Challenger
and East Kent Goldings whole hops

TASTING NOTES

Nose	Fat grain and fruit jam aromas
Palate	Sweet malt in the mouth offset by lingering hop finish with fruit notes
Comments	Dark, easy drinking beer, like a strong mild

6 **Butcombe Brewery Ltd**

**Butcombe, nr Blagdon, Bristol, Avon BS18 6XQ
Tel: 027 587 2240**

Independent
Reception centre No. *Brewery tours* trade only

BUTCOMBE BITTER

OG 1039° ABV 4%
Ingredients: 100% malt
mash: no other
information given

TASTING NOTES

Nose	Delicate floral Goldings aroma
Palate	Cleansing malt and hop in the mouth, dry, lingering finish
Comments	Subtle, beautifully-crafted, fine drinking bitter

7   Courage Ltd

Bristol Brewery, Counterslip, Bristol, Avon BS1 6EX Tel: 0272 297222

Subsidiary of Courage
Reception centre Yes. *Brewery tours* by arrangement

BITTER ALE
OG 1030° ABV 3.2%
Ingredients: pale malt,
crystal malt, black malt for
colour, brewing sugar. Wye
Target hop pellets

TASTING NOTES

Nose	Delicate hop flower aroma
Palate	Light grain in the mouth, refreshing light hop finish
Comments	Quenching, easy-drinking "boy's bitter"

BEST BITTER
OG 1039° ABV 4%
Ingredients: pale malt, crystal malt, black malt for
colour, brewing sugar. Wye Target hop pellets

TASTING NOTES

Nose	Pronounced malt and fruit aromas with light hop notes
Palate	Fat malt and toffee notes in the mouth, dry finish with some hop character
Comments	Ruby coloured decidedly malty bitter

DIRECTORS BITTER
OG 1046° ABV 4.8%
Ingredients: pale malt, crystal malt, black malt for
colour, brewing sugar. Wye Target hop pellets

TASTING NOTES

Nose	Powerful vinous attack of grain and fruit
Palate	Fat grain and fruit in the mouth, intense bitter-sweet finish
Comments	Superb, full-drinking and intriguingly complex ale; excellent with traditional English dishes. Best Bitter and Directors are sold throughout the Courage estate; Directors is also sold in John Smith's northern outlets

8 Cornish Brewery Co

**The Steam Brewery, Foundry Row, Redruth, Corn-
wall TR10 8LA Tel: 0209 213591**

Subsidiary of J.A. Devenish PLC
Reception centre Yes. *Brewery tours* Yes

JD DRY HOP BITTER
OG 1032° ABV 3.1%
Ingredients: pale malt and
crystal malt (85%), invert sugar.
Fuggles, Goldings and Progress
pellet hops

TASTING NOTES

Nose	Tempting floral hop aroma
Palate	Light balance of grain and hop, dry finish with good hop character
Comments	Refreshing, easy drinking light bitter

CORNISH ORIGINAL

OG 1038° ABV 3.6%
Ingredients: pale malt and crystal malt (85%), invert sugar. Fuggles, Goldings and Progress pellet hops

TASTING NOTES

Nose	Malt and hop bouquet with some fruit developing
Palate	Grainy mouth feel with some hop balance, dry finish with fruit notes and slight astringency
Comments	A rounded malty ale

DRAUGHT STEAM BITTER

OG 1038° ABV 3.6%
Ingredients: pale malt (100%). Fuggles, Goldings and Progress pellet hops

TASTING NOTES

Nose	Light grain and hop flower bouquet
Palate	Malt in the mouth with bitter-sweet finish
Comments	Light quenching bitter, good with fish dishes

WESSEX BITTER

OG 1042° ABV 3.9%
Ingredients: pale malt and crystal malt (85%), invert sugar. Fuggles, Goldings and Progress pellet hops

TASTING NOTES

Nose	Pronounced malt aroma

Palate	Fat grain in the mouth, rounded finish with some fruit and hop notes
Comments	Sweet premium bitter in need of more hop character

9 Cotleigh Brewery

Ford Road, Wiveliscombe, Somerset TA4 2RE
Tel: 0984 24086

Independent
Reception centre No. *Brewery tours* No

HARRIER SPA (formerly Kingfisher Ale)
OG 1036°
Ingredients: pale, crystal and chocolate malt. English whole hops

TASTING NOTES

Nose	Delicate mellow aromas of hops and honey notes
Palate	Cleansing grain and hop palate with lingering bitter-sweet finish
Comments	Fine golden bitter with pronounced floral hop character

TAWNY BITTER
OG 1040°
Ingredients: pale, crystal and chocolate malt. English whole hops

TASTING NOTES

Nose	Rich malty aroma with hop background
Palate	Smooth, rich balance of malt and hop, rounded finish with hop bitterness and fruit notes
Comments	Ripe and beautifully balanced coppery ale; superb with pasta or cheese dishes

OLD BUZZARD

OG 1048°
Ingredients: pale, crystal and chocolate malt. English whole hops

TASTING NOTES

Nose	Roast chestnut and coffee aromas
Palate	Rich chewy grain in the mouth, deep finish with hop and hints of black chocolate
Comments	Dark ruby strong beer

10 Exmoor Ales Ltd

Golden Hill Brewery, Wiveliscombe, Somerset TA4 2NY Tel: 0984 23798

Independent
Reception centre No. *Brewery tours* Yes

EXMOOR ALE

OG 1039° ABV 4%
Ingredients: pale malt
and crystal malt.
Challenger, Fuggles
and Goldings whole
hops

TASTING NOTES

Nose	Rich grain aroma
Palate	Ripe malt in the mouth with light, quenching hop finish
Comments	Good drinking session bitter

EXMOOR DARK

OG 1042° ABV 4.5%
Ingredients: pale malt and crystal malt. Challenger, Fuggles and Goldings whole hops in copper; dry hopped in cask

TASTING NOTES

Nose	Rich aromatic Goldings character with toffee notes
Comments	Flavoursome malt in the mouth, deep, dry finish with hop bitterness and vanilla notes
Comments	Complex dark ale

EXMOOR GOLD

OG 1045° ABV 4.75%
Ingredients: 100% pale malt. Challenger, Fuggles and
Goldings whole hops

TASTING NOTES

Nose	Stunning hop resin aroma with delicate butterscotch notes
Palate	Dry, quenching balance of malt and hops, long finish with bitter-sweet notes and light fruit hints
Comments	Unusual golden ale, almost a hybrid with a "lagerish" bouquet and the palate and finish of a strong ale

11   Mill Brewery

**Unit 18c, Bradley Lane, Newton Abbot, Devon
TQ12 1LZ Tel: 0626 63322**

Independent   *Reception centre* No.   *Brewery tours* No

JANNER'S ALE

OG 1038°
Ingredients: pale malt,
crystal malt and pale
chocolate malt.
Challenger and Fuggles
whole hops

TASTING NOTES

Nose	Wafting aroma of hop flower
Palate	Dry malt and chocolate hints in the mouth, deep bitter finish
Comments	Uncompromisngly dry and bitter ale

JANNER'S OLD DARK

OG 1040°
Ingredients: pale malt and black malt. Challenger and
Fuggles whole hops

TASTING NOTES

Nose	Light hop aroma with hints of roasted coffee
Palate	Rich malt in the mouth, dry finish with hop bitterness and dark chocolate
Comments	Mellow dark mild, brewed usually in summer only

JANNER'S OLD ORIGINAL

OG 1045°
Ingredients: pale malt and crystal malt. Challenger
whole hops

TASTING NOTES

Nose	Pronounced hop aroma with ripe fruit notes developing
Palate	Mouth-filling malt and hop in the mouth, deep finish with hop and fruit notes
Comments	Deceptively pale strong beer; OG increased to 1050° in winter and sold as Janner's Christmas Ale; Janner is local term for a Devonian

12   Miners Arms Brewery

**Westbury sub Mendip, Somerset
Tel: 0769 870119**

Independent
Reception centre No. *Brewery tours* Yes

OWN ALE
OG 1040°
Ingredients not
revealed* save for
Fuggles whole hops

TASTING NOTES

Nose	Delicate hop aroma with malt notes
Palate	Good rich malt in the mouth with long dry finish
Comments	As the brewer says, "a good roll-round-the-tongue bitter"

GUV'NOR'S SPECIAL BREW
OG 1048°
Ingredients not revealed* save for Goldings whole hops

TASTING NOTES

Nose	Rich grain with hop notes
Palate	Mellow malt in the mouth, smooth dry finish
Comments	Mid-brown, easy drinking ale. *Brewer says "I forget"! Despite the name, this is not a pub-brewery

13 Oakhill

**Old Brewery, High Street, Oakhill, Somerset
Tel: 0749 840134**

Independent
Reception centre No. *Brewery tours* by arrangement

FARMERS ALE

OG 1038°
Ingredients: pale malt
and crystal malt.
Bramling Cross,
Challenger, Fuggles and
Worcester Goldings
Variety whole hops

TASTING NOTES

Nose	Rich hop and grain aromas
Palate	Tasty malt in the mouth, dry quenching finish
Comments	Well-balanced no-nonsense country ale

YEOMAN ALE

OG 1050°
Ingredients: pale malt and crystal malt. Bramling
Cross, Challenger, Fuggles and Worcester Goldings
Variety whole hops

TASTING NOTES

Nose	Ripe promise of fat grain
Palate	Full malt in the mouth with deep bitter-sweet finish and vinous notes
Comments	Rounded, fine tasting copper-coloured strong ale, excellent with Stilton or other full-flavoured cheeses

14   Plympton Brewery

Furgusons Ltd, Valley Road, Plympton, Plymouth, Devon PL7 3LQ Tel: 0752 330171

Subsidiary of Allied Breweries
Reception centre No. *Brewery tours* by arrangement

PLYMPTON BEST OR DARTMOOR BEST
OG 1038° ABV 3.7%
Ingredients: pale malt (86%), crystal malt (14%).
Fuggles and Goldings whole hops

TASTING NOTES

Nose	Light hop and malt aromas
Palate	Malt in the mouth, dry finish with hint of toffee
Comments	Pleasant amber coloured ale

DARTMOOR STRONG
OG 1044° ABV 4.5%
Ingredients: pale malt (93%), crystal malt (7%). Fuggles and Goldings whole hops

TASTING NOTES

Nose	Good Goldings aroma, fruit notes developing
Palate	Full malt in the mouth, dry bitter-sweet finish with slight citric notes
Comments	Golden brew with good light balance of flavours

15 St Austell Brewery Co Ltd

**63 Trevarthian Road, St Austell, Cornwall PL25
4BY Tel: 0726 74444**

Independent
Reception centre Yes. *Brewery tours* by arrangement

BOSUN'S BITTER
OG 1034.5° ABV 3.4%
Ingredients: pale malt and
crystal malt. British
Columbian Bramlings,
Fuggles and Goldings
whole and pellet hops

TASTING NOTES

Nose	Delicate hop aroma
Palate	Light balance of malt and hop with short finish
Comments	Pleasant session light bitter

XXXX
OG 1037.5° ABV 3.6%
Ingredients: pale malt and crystal malt, caramel for
colour. British Columbian Bramlings, Fuggles and
Goldings whole and pellet hops

TASTING NOTES

Nose	Pronounced malt and roasted aromas
Palate	Sweet malt in the mouth, good dry and nutty finish
Comments	Dark, almost stout-coloured mild ale

TINNERS BITTER

OG 1038.5° ABV 3.7%
Ingredients: pale malt and crystal malt. British
Columbian Bramlings, Fuggles and Goldings whole
and pellet hops

TASTING NOTES

Nose	Light hop and buttercup bouquet
Palate	Malt, hops and light fruit in the mouth, lingering hop finish
Comments	Mellow, easy drinking bitter

HSD or HICKS SPECIAL

OG 1050.5° ABV 5%
Ingredients: pale malt and crystal malt. British
Columbian Bramlings, Fuggles and Goldings whole
hops

TASTING NOTES

Nose	Rich aromas of hop resins and pear drops
Palate	Warm biscuity flavour in mouth, long bitter-sweet finish with ripe fruit notes
Comments	Ripe, complex strong ale; HSD is known locally as "High Speed Diesel"

16 Smiles Brewing Co Ltd

Colston Yard, Colston Street, Bristol, Avon BR1 5BD Tel: 0272 297350

Independent
Reception centre Yes. *Brewery tours* by arrangement

BREWERY BITTER

OG 1037° ABV 3%
Ingredients: pale and amber malt. East Kent Goldings whole hops

TASTING NOTES

Nose	Fresh hop and crusty bread
Palate	Dry malt in the mouth, long bitter hop finish
Comments	Golden quaffing bitter

BEST BITTER

OG 1041° ABV 4%
Ingredients: pale and crystal malt. East Kent Goldings whole hops

TASTING NOTES

Nose	Rich malt bouquet with delicate Goldings aroma
Palate	Ripe malt in the mouth, long delicately dry finish
Comments	Red-brown complex bitter, good drinking companion for cheese or fish dishes

EXHIBITION BITTER

OG 1052° ABV 6%
Ingredients: pale, crystal and chocolate malt. East Kent Goldings whole hops

---

TASTING NOTES

Nose	Powerful promise of hops and fruit
Palate	Fat grain in the mouth, long bitter-sweet finish with charcoal notes
Comments	Dark fruity beer, rich and complex

OLD VIC

OG 1065° ABV 8%
Ingredients: pale, crystal and chocolate malt. East Kent Goldings whole hops

TASTING NOTES

Nose	Big bouncing bouquet of hop and fruit
Palate	Enormous malt and fruit character in mouth, rich bitter-sweet finish
Comments	Dark winter beer, a pipe and slippers job

17 Thompsons

London Inn, 11 West Street, Ashburton, Devon TQ13 7BD Tel: 0364 52478

Independent
No information received

BITTER
OG 1040°

TASTING NOTES

Nose	Rich malt aroma with some fruit developing
Palate	Fat grain and fruit in the mouth, deep dry finish
Comments	Fine, good drinking, well-balanced bitter

IPA
OG 1045°

TASTING NOTES

Nose	Powerful bouquet of sweet malt and ripe fruit
Palate	Bitter-sweet grain giving way to deep, intense dry finish with bitter hop and tart fruit notes
Comments	Complex, distinctive copper ale

WALES

At the risk of antagonising the nationalists, there is an affinity between the beers of south Wales and the English West Midlands. Both still produce substantial quantities of dark mild and the bitters have a malty sweetness. The connection is obvious: both regions are still important, if shrunken, industrial ones and in Wales workers leaving the pit or the furnace needed copious quantities of light, quaffable and sweetish beers to replace lost energy. Wales has suffered grievously from brewery closures—oh to have a brewery named Evan Evans Bevan!—and there is no beer style to discuss in north Wales because of the lack of producers, save for a few plucky micro-brewers. The long-term future of Buckley, Felinfoel and Crown is in some doubt: Guinness in the shape of the Harp lager group now has a major interest in Buckley and Crown, and Buckley in turn owns a substantial block of shares in its Llanelli neighbour of Felinfoel. As ever, the best advice in Wales is to use your Brains!

1   S.A. Brain & Co Ltd

The Old Brewery, St Mary Street, Cardiff
S. Glamorgan CF1 1SP Tel: 0222 399022

Independent
Reception centre No. *Brewery tours* strictly limited

RED DRAGON DARK
OG 1035° ABV 3.5%
Ingredients: pale malt, chocolate malt, invert and
glucose sugars. Fuggles and Goldings whole hops

TASTING NOTES

Nose	Delicate hop and faint chocolate aromas
Palate	Malt and slight nut in the mouth, light dry finish
Comments	Rich ruby mild, good tasting and eminently quaffable

BITTER or LIGHT
OG 1035° ABV 3.7%
Ingredients: pale malt, crystal malt, invert and glucose
sugars. Fuggles and Goldings whole hops

TASTING NOTES

Nose	Fragrant promise of malt and hops
Palate	Grain character in the mouth, quenching lightly hopped finish
Comments	Refreshing amber light bitter

SA BEST BITTER
OG 1042° ABV 4.2%
Ingredients: pale malt,
crystal malt, invert
and glucose sugars. Fuggles
and Goldings whole hops

TASTING NOTES

Nose	Booming hop and grain aromas with fruit notes
Palate	Big round grainy mouth-feel, deep bitter-sweet finish
Comments	Superb deep amber beer, known to aficionados as "Skull Attack"

2   Bullmastiff

5 Anchor Way, Penarth, S. Glamorgan CF6 1SF Tel: 0222 702985

No information received

BITTER
OG 1035°

TASTING NOTES

Nose	Tempting hop resin aroma
Palate	Fine balance of grain and hop with deep dry finish
Comments	Quenching and tasty session bitter

EBONY DARK
OG 1042°

TASTING NOTES

Nose	Rich bouquet of roast malt and hop
Palate	Intense mouth feel of chewy dark grain, dry finish with hop and vanilla notes
Comments	Luscious dark beer

BEST BITTER
OG 1043

TASTING NOTES

Nose	Delicate aromas of grain, hop and some fruit
Palate	Bitter-sweet grain and hop in the mouth, light dry finish with some tangy fruit notes
Comments	Fine cleansing bitter

SON OF A BITCH
OG 1062°

TASTING NOTES

Nose	Rich and ripe malt and hop bouquet
Palate	Vinous mix of grain and fruit with deep, rounded bitter-sweet finish
Comments	Complex strong brew

3   Crown Buckley

The Brewery, Gilbert Road, Llanelli, Dyfed. *Head office:* **Crown Brewery, Pontyclun, Mid Glamorgan Tel: 0554 758441**

A partnership of Crown and the Harp Consortium
Reception centre Yes. *Brewery tours* Trade and CAMRA groups only

BUCKLEY'S MILD
or DARK or 4X

OG 1032° ABV 3.3%
Ingredients: Maris Otter
pale malt, 8% black malt,
wheat malt and flaked
maize. Challenger,
Fuggles, Goldings and
Worcester Goldings
Variety hop pellets with
small % Hallertau
Brewers Gold

TASTING NOTES

Nose	Lush roast malt and chocolate aromas
Palate	Good tasty, chewy grain in the mouth, dry earthy finish with light hop and chocolate notes
Comments	Splendid tasty dark mild

BUCKLEY BEST BITTER
OG 1036° ABV 3.8%
Ingredients: Maris Otter pale malt, 8% wheat malt and flaked maize. Challenger, Fuggles, Goldings and Worcester Goldings Variety hop pellets with small % of Hallertau Brewers Gold

TASTING NOTES

Nose	Pleasing bouquet of malt and hop

Palate	Rounded grain in the mouth, full, deep finish with good hop and nut character
Comments	Balanced good drinking session bitter

CROWN SBB or SPECIAL BEST BITTER

OG 1037° ABV 3.8%
Ingredients: Maris Otter pale malt, 11% wheat and flaked barley. Bramling Cross, Fuggles and Goldings whole hops, small % Saaz

TASTING NOTES

Nose	Fruity, estery aroma
Palate	Mellow malt in the mouth, rich, deep finish with hop and ripe fruit notes
Comments	A tangy, distinctive ale

CROWN 1041

OG 1041%
Ingredients: Maris Otter pale malt, 14% crystal malt and flaked maize. Bramling Cross, Fuggles and Goldings whole hops, small % Saaz

TASTING NOTES

Nose	Powerful malt and ripe fruit aromas
Palate	Rich malt and fruit with hop edge, intense complex finish of hop and tart fruit
Comments	A ripe, coppery, full-tasting ale. Crown closed in summer 1989 with production transferred to Buckley.

4   Felinfoel Brewery Ltd

Felinfoel, Llanelli, Dyfed SA14 8LB
Tel: 0554 773357

Independent
Reception centre No. *Brewery tours* No

FELINFOEL BEST BITTER
OG 1032° ABV 3.3%
Ingredients: Triumph pale malt (85%), torrefied
wheat (15%), invert sugar. Bramling Cross,
Challenger and Fuggles whole hops

TASTING NOTES

Nose	Deep grain and toast nose
Palate	Nutty malt in the mouth, fragrant hop flower finish
Comments	Superb pale bitter with a fine balance of flavours; delightful companion for shell fish or light cheeses

DOUBLE DRAGON
OG 1040° ABV 4%
Ingredients: Triumph pale
malt (85%), torrefied wheat
(15%), invert sugar.
Bramling Cross, Challenger
and Fuggles whole hops

TASTING NOTES

Nose	Big malt and yeasty aromas, hop notes developing
Palate	Cleansing grain and hop in the mouth, deep, complex finish with hop, lemon drops and faint toffee notes
Comments	Beautifully crafted golden bitter

5 Pembrokeshire's Own Ales Ltd

Llanteglos Brewery, Llanteg, Narberth, Dyfed SA67 8PU Tel: 083 483 677

Independent
Reception centre Yes. *Brewery tours* Yes

BENFRO BITTER
OG 1036° ABV 3.8%
Ingredients: Maris Otter pale malt, crystal malt,
torrefied wheat (10%). Goldings and Hallertau whole
hops

TASTING NOTES

Nose	Tangy aromas of hops and light citric fruit
Palate	Mellow malt and honey with light dry finish
Comments	Pale, smooth-drinking session bitter

BENFRO EXTRA
OG 1041° ABV 4.3%
Ingredients: Maris Otter pale
malt, crystal malt, torrefied
wheat (10%). Goldings and
Hallertau whole hops

TASTING NOTES

Nose	Rich grain and nut bouquet
Palate	Sweet malt and cob nuts in the mouth, deep, dry finish
Comments	Good drinking russet ale. Benfro is Welsh for the old country of Pembroke

6   Plassey Brewery

Eyton, Wrexham, Clwyd LL13 0SP
Tel: 0978 780922

Independent
Reception centre Yes. *Brewery tours* Small parties by
arrangement

FARMHOUSE BITTER

OG 1039° ABV 3.6%
Ingredients: 100% pale malt,
small amount of coloured sugar.
Fuggles whole hops

TASTING NOTES

Nose	Light hop bouquet
Palate	Rounded malt in the mouth, long dry finish with fruit notes
Comments	Pale, refreshing bitter; brewed in an old dairy, sold in bar of neighbouring caravan site and few local outlets

7   Sam Powell Brewery

Unit 14, Mochdre Industrial Estate, Newtown,
Powys SY16 4LD Tel: 0686 628021

Independent
Reception centre No. *Brewery tours* No

BEST BITTER
OG 1034° ABV 3%
Ingredients: pale malt (86%),
crystal malt (5.5%), chocolate
malt (1%), wheat flour (7.5%).
Fuggles and Goldings whole
hops

TASTING NOTES

Nose	Delicate Goldings bouquet
Palate	Light grain in the mouth, clean hop finish
Comments	Pale, refreshing session bitter

ORIGINAL BITTER
OG 1038° ABV 3.5%
Ingredients: pale malt (86%), crystal malt (5.5%),
chocolate malt (1%), wheat flour (7.5%). Fuggles and
Goldings whole hops

TASTING NOTES

Nose	Rich tang of hops and grain
Palate	Full malt in the mouth with deep bitter finish and some light fruit notes
Comments	Good rounded, deep-drinking bitter

SAMSON ALE
OG 1048° ABV 4.3%
Ingredients: pale malt (86.5%), crystal malt (5.5%),
chocolate malt (1%), wheat flour (7%). Fuggles and
Goldings whole hops

TASTING NOTES

Nose	Dry roast malt aroma
Palate	Ripe winey flavour with hop bitter edge, dry finish with distinct chocolate notes
Comments	Dark copper ale full of good chewy grain character

8   Welsh Brewers Ltd

Crawshay Street, Cardiff, S Glam CF1 1TR
Tel: 0222 233071

Subsidiary of Bass
Reception centre Yes. *Brewery tours* by arrangement

WORTHINGTON PA; HANCOCK'S PA; WORTHINGTON M

The same brew but priming sugar is added in different amounts
OG 1033° ABV 3.3%
Ingredients: pale malt, copper sugars, sucrose as priming sugar. Challenger, Northdown and other hop varieties in pellet form

TASTING NOTES

Nose	Light malt and hop aroma
Palate	Delicate grain in the mouth, slight hop finish
Comments	Session bitters with slight variations in palate but lightly hopped

HANCOCK'S HB

OG 1037° ABV 3.8%
Ingredients: pale malt, copper sugars, sucrose as priming sugar. Challenger, Northdown and other hop varieties in pellet form

TASTING NOTES

Nose	Light malt and hop aroma
Palate	Sweet malt in the mouth, light dry finish
Comments	Pleasant, refreshing but undemanding bitter

WORTHINGTON DARK

OG 1034° ABV 3.3%
Ingredients: pale malt, copper sugars, sucrose as
priming sugar. Challenger, Northdown and other hop
varieties in pellet form

TASTING NOTES

Nose	Grainy aroma
Palate	Chewy malt in the mouth, short bitter-sweet finish
Comments	Malty, creamy mild

WORTHINGTON BB

OG 1037° ABV 3.8%
Ingredients: pale malt, copper sugars, sucrose as
priming sugar. Challenger, Northdown and other hop
varieties in pellet form

TASTING NOTES

Nose	Malt aroma with slight hop notes
Palate	Grain in thc mouth with light, dry finish and some hop character
Comments	Pale, easy quaffing light bitter with little hop character

NORTH-WEST ENGLAND

North-west England, a region of great industrial
cities as well as fine countryside and the tranquil
beauty of the Lake District, has breweries in
profusion, though here as in the rest of Britain
takeover attrition is whittling the numbers. There is
still a fine choice, though, with beers that range
from the almost lagerish pale gold of Boddington's
renowned bitter to darker brews, including several
still surviving milds. There are some malty ales but
the tendency is towards dry, fruity and even tart
bitters. Manchester is a remarkable city for choice,
with independent brewers who have survived the
clutches of the giants and who produce not only
beers of great quality but which are also remarkable
value for money.

1 Boddingtons Breweries Ltd

Strangeways Brewery, PO Box 331, Greater Manchester M60 3EL Tel: 061-831 7881

Independent
Reception centre Yes. *Brewery tours* Yes

BODDINGTONS MILD

OG 1032° ABV 3.1%
Ingredients: pale malt (85%), crystal malt (9%), chocolate malt (2%), cane sugar (4%), trace of caramel. Primed with cane sugar. Bramling Cross, British Columbian, Fuggles, Goldings and Whitbread Goldings Variety whole hops

TASTING NOTES

Nose	Light fruit and roasted grain aromas
Palate	Chewy dark grain in the mouth, light finish with dark chocolate notes
Comments	Pleasant, easy-drinking tawny ale

OB MILD

OG 1032° ABV 3.1%
Ingredients: pale malt (85%), crystal malt (9%), chocolate malt (2%), cane sugar (4%), trace of caramel. Primed with cane sugar. British Columbian, Fuggles and Goldings whole hops

TASTING NOTES

Nose	Slight roasted grain notes
Palate	Grain and chocolate in the mouth, light hop and nut finish
Comments	Darkish mild, hard to distinguish from its mild stablemate

BODDINGTONS BITTER

OG 1035° ABV 3.8%

Ingredients: pale malt (95.5%), patent malt (1.5%), cane sugar (3%). Primed with cane sugar. Bramling Cross (8%), Fuggles (35%), Goldings (30%), Northern Brewer (5%) and Whitbread Goldings Variety (22%) whole hops

TASTING NOTES

Nose	Complex floral, lemon jelly and spice aromas
Palate	Flinty dryness in the mouth, long hard finish with hop bitterness and tart fruit
Comments	A remarkable light golden bitter, a fine quenching session ale or excellent with fish dishes. The brewer detects slight brandy notes on the nose

OB BITTER

OG 1038° ABV 3.8%
Ingredients: pale malt (87%), crystal malt (5%), cane sugar (8%), trace of caramel. Primed with cane sugar. British Columbian, Fuggles, Goldings and Styrian Goldings whole hops

TASTING NOTES

Nose	Heady bouquet of malt and hops with fruit notes developing
Palate	Big, round malt and fruit in mouth with deep bitter-sweet finish
Comments	Hearty, rounded dark golden ale, splendid with crusty bread and mellow cheese. OB in the names of the mild and bitter refer to the Oldham Brewery, bought and closed by Boddingtons

2 Matthew Brown Ltd

PO Box 5, Lion Brewery, Blackburn, Lancs BB1 5NH Tel: 0254 52471

Subsidiary of Scottish & Newcastle Breweries
Reception centre Yes. *Brewery tours* Yes

MILD

OG 1032° ABV 3.1%
Ingredients: pale malt,
crystal malt, wheat, maize,
cane sugar, caramel for
colour. Goldings and Fuggles
whole and pellet hops

TASTING NOTES

Nose	Light grain and coffee aromas
Palate	Chewy dark, nutty malt with short dry finish with chocolate notes
Comments	Pleasant dark mild

BITTER

OG 1035° ABV 3.5%
Ingredients: pale malt, wheat, maize, cane sugar.
Fuggles and Goldings whole and pellet hops

TASTING NOTES

Nose	Mellow malt with hop background
Palate	Smooth malt in the mouth, light bitter-sweet finish
Comments	Creamy, easy-drinking bitter

3   Burtonwood Brewery PLC

Burtonwood Village, nr Warrington, Cheshire WA5 4PJ Tel: 09252 5131

Independent
Reception centre Yes. *Brewery tours* Parties only by arrangement

DARK MILD

OG 1032° ABV 2.9%
Ingredients: pale malt (70%), crystal malt (7%), black malt (2%), torrefied wheat (9%), invert sugar (10%), caramel (2%). Challenger, Fuggles, Progress and Worcester Goldings Variety whole hops

TASTING NOTES

Nose	Rich aroma of burnt toast with hop notes developing
Palate	Rich nutty grain in the mouth, good hop finish
Comments	Fine example of a characterful dark mild

BITTER

OG 1036° ABV 3.7%
Ingredients: pale malt (65%), crystal malt (6%), torrefied wheat (10%), invert sugar (19%). Challenger, Fuggles, Progress and Worcester Goldings Variety

TASTING NOTES

Nose	Fine aromatic bouquet of hop resin and nutty grain

Palate	Mellow malt in the mouth with yeast notes, long finish full of hop character
Comments	Delectable, underrated quality bitter

4 Greenalls Ltd

Wilderspool Brewery, PO Box 2, Warrington, Cheshire WA4 6RH Tel: 0925 51234

Part of the Greenall Whitley group
Reception centre Yes. *Brewery tours* Yes

CASK MILD
OG 1033° ABV 3.2%
Ingredients: malt (93%), wheat flour (7%). Fuggles and Goldings hop pellets

TASTING NOTES

Nose	Light hop and dark malt aroma
Palate	Full sweet grain in the mouth, light bitter finish with hint of nut
Comments	Creamy, lightly hopped dark mild

CASK BITTER
OG 1036° ABV 3.8%
Ingredients: malt (90%), wheat flour (10%). Fuggles and Goldings hop pellets

TASTING NOTES

Nose	Background aromas of malt and hop
Palate	Light balance of grain and hop in the mouth, clean, dry finish
Comments	Smooth but somewhat bland quaffing ale

THOMAS GREENALL'S ORIGINAL BITTER

OG 1045° ABV 5%
Ingredients: malt and maltose syrup (no %). Fuggles
and Goldings hop pellets

TASTING NOTES

Nose	Complex aromas of oranges and lemons, hops and slight sulphur
Palate	Delicate grain in the mouth, dry finish with blackcurrant notes
Comments	Soft, easy-drinking, fruity tawny bitter

5   Hartleys (Ulverston) Ltd

**Old Brewery, Ulverston, Cumbria LA12 7HX
Tel 0229 53269**

Subsidiary of Frederic Robinson Ltd of Stockport
Reception centre No. *Brewery tours* by arrangement

MILD

OG 1031° ABV 3.1%
Ingredients not revealed

TASTING NOTES

Nose	Gentle hop and nutty grain
Palate	Chewy malt and caramel in the mouth, dry finish with hop and coffee notes
Comments	Smooth, easy-drinking dark mild

BITTER
OG 1031° ABV 3.1%
Ingredients not revealed

TASTING NOTES

Nose	Delicate hop aroma
Palate	Light grain in the mouth, short finish with good hop notes
Comments	Easy drinking, well hopped for its gravity

FELLRUNNERS
OG 1035° ABV 3.5%
Ingredients not revealed

TASTING NOTES

Nose	Fine, tempting hop aroma
Palate	Rounded malt in the mouth with bitter hop edge, long finish with hop and fruit notes
Comments	A good tawny bitter with pronounced hop character

XB
OG 1040° ABV 4%
Ingredients not revealed

TASTING NOTES

Nose	Warm aromas of rich grain and hops
Palate	Rounded malt and hop in the mouth, long dry finish with citric fruit notes developing
Comments	A fine, beautifully balanced premium bitter with slight but not displeasing astringency in the finish; splendid with fish

6 Higsons Ltd

The Brewery, Stanhope Street, Liverpool, Merseyside L8 5XJ Tel: 051-709 8734

Subsidiary of Boddingtons Breweries Ltd
Reception centre Yes. *Brewery tours* Yes

MILD

OG 1033° ABV 3.1%
Ingredients: mild malt (71%), crystal malt (6%), wheat (11%), invert sugar (12%), trace of caramel. Primed with cane sugar. Bramling Cross, British Columbian, Fuggles, Goldings and Whitbread Goldings Variety hop pellets

TASTING NOTES

Nose	Warm breakfast aromas of toast and coffee
Palate	Dry nutty grain in the mouth, dry finish with some hop notes
Comments	Port-wine coloured, tasty and chewy mild

BITTER

OG 1038° ABV 3.8%
Ingredients: pale malt (85.5%), crystal malt (3%), wheat (3.5%), invert sugar (8%), trace of caramel. Primed with cane sugar. Bramling Cross, British Columbian, Fuggles, Goldings, Styrian Goldings and Whitbread Goldings Variety

TASTING NOTES

Nose	Massive Goldings bouquet and some tart fruit notes
Palate	Flinty balance of hop and grain, intense bitter finish
Comments	Stunning, uncompromisingly bitter golden brew of great character

Joseph Holt & Co Ltd

Derby Brewery, Empire Street, Cheetham, Manchester M3 1JD Tel: 061-834 3285

Independent
No information received

MILD
OG 1033°

TASTING NOTES

Nose	Dry grain, hop and chocolate notes
Palate	Light balance of malt and hop, complex bitter-sweet finish with hop and black chocolate notes
Comments	Potable dark mild with good hop character

BITTER
OG 1039°

TASTING NOTES

Nose	Superb hop bouquet with tart fruit notes
Palate	Quenching balance of malt and hop, cleansing delicate finish with some citric fruit
Comments	A bitter of great distinction and drinkability

8   Hydes' Anvil Brewery Ltd

**46 Moss Lane West, Manchester M15 5PH
Tel: 061-226 1317**

Independent
Reception centre Yes. *Brewery tours* by arrangement

ANVIL MILD

OG 1032° ABV 3%
Ingredients: 100% malt,
caramel for colour 0.05%.
Fuggles and Goldings whole hops

TASTING NOTES

Nose	Gentle grain and hop
Palate	Malty in the mouth, short delicate finish
Comments	A pleasant, refreshing ruby coloured mild

ANVIL LIGHT

OG 1034° ABV 3.5%
Ingredients: 100% malt, caramel for colour 0.025%.
Fuggles and Goldings whole hops

TASTING NOTES

Nose	Delicate promise of hop
Palate	Light quenching balance of malt and hop, cleansing finish
Comments	A light amber-coloured mild

ANVIL BITTER

OG 1036° ABV 4%
Ingredients: 100% pale malt. Fuggles and Goldings
whole hops

TASTING NOTES

Nose	Rich hop resin aroma with slight tart fruit notes

Palate	Full malt and hop in the mouth with dry, crisp finish
Comments	Succulent, fine drinking bitter that suggests more than its gravity

ANVIL STRONG ALE or XXXX

OG 1080° ABV 7.5%
Ingredients: 100% pale malt, caramel for colour
0.075%. Fuggles and Goldings whole hops

TASTING NOTES

Nose	Heady aromas of fruit, sweet malt and hops
Palate	Hearty flavours of malt and fruit, deep, rounded finish with complex balance of hop bitterness and raisins and sultanas
Comments	A big, warming, rich winter brew; pass the walnuts!

Jennings Bros PLC

**Castle Brewery, Cockermouth, Cumbria CA13 9NE
Tel: 0900 823214**

Independent
Reception centre Yes. *Brewery tours* by arrangement

MILD

OG 1034°
Ingredients not revealed

TASTING NOTES

Nose	Nutty, malty aromas with delicate hop notes
Palate	Rich grainy flavours with well-balanced mellow finish
Comments	Dark mild full of good biscuity flavours with hop balance

BITTER

OG 1035° ABV 3.4%
Ingredients: pale malt (85%), wheat and syrups
(15%). Bramling Cross, Challenger, Fuggles and
Goldings whole hops

TASTING NOTES

Nose	Complex bouquet of tangy hop resin and rich malt
Palate	Pronounced, deep flavours of rich malt and hop bitterness, long tart finish
Comments	A brilliantly distinctive coppery bitter with a lactic sourness in the finish

10   J.W. Lees & Co Ltd

Greengate Brewery, Middleton Junction, Manchester M24 2AX Tel: 061-643 2487

Independent
Reception centre No. *Brewery tours* Yes

GB MILD

OG 1032° ABV 3%
Ingredients: Maris Otter pale malt
and invert sugar. Fuggles and East
Kent Goldings whole and pellet hops

TASTING NOTES

Nose	Sweet malt aroma
Palate	Good grain flavours in the mouth, dry, nutty finish
Comments	Tasty, earthy medium dark mild

BITTER

OG 1038° ABV 4%
Ingredients: Maris Otter pale malt, caramel for colour adjustment. Fuggles and East Kent Goldings whole and pellet hops

TASTING NOTES

Nose	Lilting Goldings bouquet
Palate	Rich malt in the mouth balanced by dry, bitter finish with hints of fruit and nut
Comments	Distinctive robust bitter, less tartly bitter than other Mancunian brews

MOONRAKER

OG 1073° ABV 7.5%
Ingredients: Maris Otter pale malt, caramel for colour adjustment. Fuggles and East Kent Goldings whole and pellet hops

TASTING NOTES

Nose	Ripe vinous attack
Palate	Big malt and hop prickle in the mouth, intense bitter-sweet finish with rich fruit notes
Comments	Deep, warming winter barley wine named after yokels who, after imbibing, attempted to rake the moon with pitchforks

1   Mitchells

11 Moor Lane, Lancaster LA1 1QB
Tel: 0524 63773/6000

Independent
No information received

MILD
OG 1033°

TASTING NOTES

Nose	Good grain and faint toffee aroma
Palate	Creamy malt in the mouth, light dry finish
Comments	Easy-drinking, mellow mild

BITTER
OG 1035°

TASTING NOTES

Nose	Hop resin and grain bouquet
Palate	Good malt and nut in the mouth, quenching dry, nutty finish
Comments	Golden refreshing brew

ESB
OG 1050°

TASTING NOTES

Nose	Powerful smack of malt, hop and fruit
Palate	Big grain and fruit in the mouth, deep hop and fruit finish
Comments	Mellow strong ale of great depth and complexity

12   Moorhouses Brewery (Burnley) Ltd

**Moorhouse Street, Burnley, Lancs BB11 5EN
Tel: 0282 22864**

Independent
Reception centre No. *Brewery tours* by arrangement

PREMIER BITTER

OG 1036° ABV 3%
Ingredients: pale malt (96%), crystal malt (4%).
Bramling Cross, Challenger, Fuggles and Goldings
whole and pellet hops

TASTING NOTES

Nose	Light bouquet of malt and Goldings hop
Palate	Delicate cleansing balance of grain and hop, good finish with hop bitterness and hint of nut
Comments	Fine tasting bitter, winner of silver medal at 1983 Brewex

PENDLE WITCHES BREW

OG 1050° ABV 5%
Ingredients: pale malt
(96%), crystal malt
(4%). Bramling Cross,
Challenger, Fuggles
and Goldings whole
and pellet hops

TASTING NOTES

Nose	Big malt and fruit bouquet
Palate	Fat sweet grain in the mouth, deep dry finish with good hop character and vanilla notes
Comments	Deceptively pale strong bitter, dangerously potable

13   Oak

**59 Merseyton Road, Ellesmere Port, South Wirral
L65 2AW Tel: 051-356 0950**

Independent
No information received

OAK BEST BITTER
OG 1038°

TASTING NOTES

Nose	Tangy bouquet of hop and grain
Palate	Superb balance of malt and hop in the mouth, tart bitter-sweet finish
Comments	Clean tasting, refreshing bitter

OLD OAK ALE
OG 1044°

TASTING NOTES

Nose	Rich malt aroma with hop and light fruit notes developing
Palate	Fat grain in the mouth with bitter hop edge, long dry finish with fine hop and fruit character
Comments	Delectable premium bitter with excellent hop balance

DOUBLE DAGGER
OG 1050°

TASTING NOTES

Nose	Pronounced ripe malt and fruit aroma
Palate	Great depth of grain in the mouth offset by dry finish with flinty hop and sharp fruit notes
Comments	Complex superior strong ale, superb with strong cheese or shell fish

WOBBLY BOB
OG 1060°

TASTING NOTES

Nose	Stunning bouquet of hop resin and ripe fruit
Palate	Enormous vinous grain and fruit in the mouth, robust dry finish with bursts of hop and fruit
Comments	Dangerously potable strong alc of great character and complexity; Oak also brews a winter Porter (1050°); not tasted

4 Frederic Robinson & Co Ltd

Unicorn Brewery, Stockport, Cheshire SK1 1JJ
Tel: 061-480 6571

Independent
Reception centre Yes. *Brewery tours* by arrangement

BEST MILD

OG 1032°
Ingredients: pale malt and
"some adjuncts".
Goldings hops and small
% of Hallertau. Dry
hopped in cask with
Goldings

Robinson's

TASTING NOTES

Nose	Light malt aroma
Palate	Delicate grain in the mouth, cleansing balance of hop in finish
Comments	Pleasant light mild; caramel is added for Dark Mild

BITTER

OG 1035°
Ingredients: pale malt and "some adjuncts". Goldings
hops and small % of Hallertau. Dry hopped in cask
with Goldings

TASTING NOTES

Nose	Delicate hop resin
Palate	Quenching light balance of grain and hop, light bitter-sweet finish
Comments	Good light session bitter, sold in only a handful of outlets

BEST BITTER

OG 1041°
Ingredients: pale malt and "some adjuncts". Goldings
hops and small % of Hallertau. Dry hopped in cask
with Goldings

TASTING NOTES

Nose	Rich complex bouquet of hop, malt and tangy fruit

Palate	Delightful mouth feel of rich malt with hop balance, long dry finish with citric notes

Comments	Superb pale, tartly quenching complex brew; one for the desert island

OLD TOM

OG 1080°
Ingredients: pale malt and "some adjuncts". Goldings and small % of Hallertau

TASTING NOTES

Nose	Heady vinous aromas of fresh leather and pickled walnuts

Palate	Booming balance of fat malt and hop prickle, deep, intense port wine finish with bitter hop balance

Comments	Dark, rich, warming superior barley wine

5   Tetley Walker Ltd

The Brewery, Dallam Lane, Warrington, Cheshire WA2 7NU Tel: 0925 31231

Subsidiary of Allied Breweries
Reception centre Yes. *Brewery tours* by arrangement
*Two of the main beers brewed are Tetley Mild and Tetley Bitter, oddly called "classic Yorkshire beers". They are replicas of the Joshua Tetley ales brewed in Leeds. To add to the confusion—but the drinkers' pleasure—the Warrington brewery has added Tetley Dark Mild. It also brews beers under the Peter Walker name for pubs in the Merseyside area.

TETLEY DARK MILD
OG 1032° ABV 2.9%
Ingredients not revealed

TASTING NOTES

Nose	Light grain and nut aromas
Palate	Chewy malt in the mouth, sweet finish with hint of hop
Comments	Pleasant dark mild

WALKER MILD
OG 1032° ABV 2.9%
Ingredients not revealed

TASTING NOTES

Nose	Delicate malt and hint of hop
Palate	Dark chewy malt in the mouth, good bitterness and fruit hints in the finish
Comments	A fascinatingly complex brew with good hop and fruit characteristics

WALKER BITTER
OG 1033° ABV 3.3%
Ingredients not revealed

TASTING NOTES

Nose	Light promise of hop
Palate	Cleansing flavours of grain and hop with good dry finish
Comments	A quenching, pleasant session bitter

WALKER BEST BITTER
OG 1036° ABV 3.3%
Ingredients not revealed

TASTING NOTES

Nose	Tangy hop resin and malt aromas
Palate	Sharp quenching balance of grain and hop, dry finish with hop and citric notes
Comments	A flinty, refreshing brew, similar to Tetley Bitter. The brewery also produces Walker Winter Warmer (1060°); not tasted

16   Daniel Thwaites PLC

PO Box 50, Star Brewery, Blackburn, Lancs BB1 5BU Tel: 0254 54431

Independent
Reception centre Yes. *Brewery tours* Yes

MILD
OG 1031° ABV 3%

Ingredients: pale malt and crystal malt (85%), copper sugar (15%). Fuggles, East Kent Goldings and Goldings blend whole hops

TASTING NOTES

Nose	Pleasing aromas of light grain and nut
Palate	Malt in the mouth, short dry finish
Comments	Easy drinking medium dark mild

BEST MILD

OG 1034° ABV 3.2%
Ingredients: pale malt and crystal malt (85%), copper
sugar (15%). Fuggles, East Kent Goldings and high
alpha Goldings blend whole hops

TASTING NOTES

Nose	Rich malt and slight nut
Palate	Mellow malt giving way to deep finish with good hop notes and chewy nut
Comments	Superb dark mild with great depth

BITTER

OG 1036° ABV 3.5%
Ingredients: pale malt (85%), copper sugar (15%).
Fuggles, East Kent Goldings, blend of various high
alpha whole hops

TASTING NOTES

Nose	Delicate bouquet of malt with hop notes developing
Palate	Mellow creamy grain with underlying hop edge, deep bitter-sweet finish with hint of nut
Comments	Superb amber beer, the archetypal North West bitter with creamy mellow malt offset by good hopping; try a mixed pint of Best Mild and Bitter

17 Yates

Ghyll Farm, Westnewton, Aspatria, Carlisle, Cumbria CA5 3NX Tel: 0965 21081

Independent
Reception centre No. *Brewery tours* No

BITTER
OG 1035° ABV 3.9%
Ingredients not revealed

TASTING NOTES

Nose	Spicy aromas of hop resin and tart fruit
Palate	Tangy balance of grain and hop, deep, intensely dry finish with good hop bitterness and light fruit
Comments	A fine straw-coloured bitter, exceptionally dry and well-attenuated. Yates also brew a bottled Premium occasionally available on draught (1039°) and Best Cellar (1052°)

NORTHERN IRELAND

Northern Ireland, not unexpectedly, is the subject of two disparate beer styles. Stout and the unremarkable keg beers of the Republic are imported while the Belfast outpost of the Bass empire concentrates on English versions of keg and lager, though it is now experimenting with its cask 80 shilling from Scotland. Hilden is the only supplier of cask conditioned beer in the province and has survived the vicissitudes of the free trade and an absence of cellars in many bars since 1981. The original brewer at Hilden, Brendan Dobbin, told me that Hilden Ale was his attempt to reproduce Fuller's London Pride as he held the Chiswick beer in such high regard, but the recipe and flavour have undergone some changes since his time at the brewery.

1 Hilden Brewery

Hilden House, Grand Street, Hilden, Lisburn, Co Antrim Tel: 0846 663863

Independent
Reception centre Yes. *Brewery tours* by arrangement

HILDEN ALE

OG 1040°
Ingredients: pale malt and
crystal malt. Goldings and
Hallertau hops

TASTING NOTES

Nose	Fragrant Goldings hop bouquet
Palate	Full bitter flavour in the mouth with dry finish and good hop character
Comments	Superb, quenching golden bitter

SPECIAL RESERVE

OG 1044°
Ingredients: pale, crystal and black malt. Goldings and
Hallertau hops

TASTING NOTES

Nose	Delicate hop aroma
Palate	Fine balance of grain and hop in the mouth, lingering bitter finish
Comments	Fine copper-coloured ale

ISLE OF MAN

The small island midway between England and
Ireland has a way of life reminiscent of the mainland
in the 1950s though it is sadly up to date in the ways
of brewery closures. The old, slightly ramshackle
Castletown Brewery, overlooking the harbour and
castle in the town of the same name, was merged
with the larger Okell Brewery of Douglas in 1986.
Okell (pronounced as in yokel, no pun intended) is
an impressive, highly professional operation and it
continues to brew Castletown Bitter, a fruity,
slightly acidic beer that is quite different in palate to
Okell's mellower mild and bitter. All the beers are
produced under the strict Manx Pure Beer Act
which permits only malt, hops, yeast, water and
minute amounts of brewing sugar (used only in
mild); mainland brewers please copy!

Isle of Man Breweries Ltd

**Falcon Brewery, Douglas, IoM
Tel: 0624 73034**

Independent
Reception centre Yes. *Brewery tours* by arrangement

OKELLS MILD

OG 1034.5° ABV 3.5%
Ingredients: Golden
Promise/Triumph pale
malt (95%), black invert
sugar, caramel for colour.
Fuggles whole hops plus
either Bramling Cross,
Northern Brewer or
Target

TASTING NOTES

Nose	Light malt
Palate	Creamy malt in the mouth, light sweet finish with hint of hop
Comments	Easy drinking dark mild

OKELLS BITTER

OG 1035.8° ABV 3.8%
Ingredients: Golden Promise/Triumph pale malt,
crystal malt. Fuggles and Goldings whole hops plus
either Bramling Cross, Northern Brewer or Target

TASTING NOTES

Nose	Rich bouquet of malt and hops
Palate	Full, rounded mellow malt in the mouth with bitter-sweet finish and light fruit notes
Comments	Smooth, creamy, easy drinking bitter

CASTLETOWN BITTER

OG 1035.8° ABV 3.9%
Ingredients: Golden Promise/Triumph pale malt,
crystal malt. Fuggles and Goldings whole hops, plus
either Bramling Cross, Northern Brewer or Target

TASTING NOTES

Nose	Tangy bouquet of hop resin and citric fruit
Palate	Sharp, quenching balance of grain and hop, dry, sharp finish with fruit notes
Comments	Superb clean-tasting aromatic pale bitter that deserves wider recognition

GUERNSEY

The Channel Islands are an oddity, close to the
French coast, speaking a patois based on Norman
French with a Hampshire accent and with a good
English ale tradition. The breweries on the major
island of Jersey produce only keg beers (though
visitors will find many outlets serving Draught Bass)
but Guernsey has two breweries which produce
cask beers of impressive quality, aided by the fact
that excise duty is payable on quantity and not
gravity. In the 1970s Guernsey, known as Pony
Ales, and Randalls, known as Bobby Ales, bowed
belatedly to the mainland wind and called their
bitters "keg" though they were in fact cask beers
served under a top pressure of gas. Now they serve
them by handpump in a minority of their outlets.
There is still a substantial demand from older locals
for malty dark mild. The Guernsey Brewery has the
grim distinction of having been taken over by the
occupying German forces in World War II; when
barley ran out, the Germans used sugar beet and
brought in equipment to produce
bottom-fermenting "lager" beer. More worryingly,
the company has been taken over by Ann Street
Brewery of Jersey, which is committed to keg beer
production. Guernsey beers are also available on
Alderney and Herm. The island of Guernsey is
"dry" on Sunday.

1   Guernsey Brewery Co (1920) Ltd

**South Esplanade, St Peter Port, Guernsey, CI
Tel: 0481 20143**

Subsidiary of Ann Street Brewery Co
Reception centre Yes. *Brewery tours* Yes

LBA MILD

OG 1038° ABV 3.7%
Ingredients: 98% malt,
flaked barley (1½%),
wheat malt, caramel for
colour. Bavarian, Fuggles
and Northern Brewer
whole and pellet hops, dry
hopped with East Kent
Goldings

TASTING NOTES

Nose	Light malt and hop aromas
Palate	Sweet malt and toffee in the mouth, dry, bitter-sweet finish
Comments	A fuller dark mild than is usual on the mainland

REAL DRAUGHT BITTER

OG 1046° ABV 4.1%
Ingredients: 98% malt, flaked barley (1½%), wheat
malt, caramel for colour. Fuggles, Hallertau and
Worcester Goldings Variety whole and pellet hops,
dry hopped with East Kent Goldings

TASTING NOTES

Nose	Rich, resiny hop bouquet
Palate	Round balance of malt and hop with long dry finish and fruit notes
Comments	Distinguished amber ale

2   R.W. Randall Ltd

Vauxlaurens Brewery, St Julian's Avenue, Guernsey CI Tel: 0481 20134

Independent
Reception centre Yes. *Brewery tours* by arrangement

BEST MILD

OG 1033°
Ingredients: pale
malt (93%), wheat
malt (3%), sugars
(4%). Fuggles whole
hops and hop oil

TASTING NOTES

Nose	Good grainy aroma
Palate	Mellow, rounded malt with hint of toffee, short dry finish
Comments	Smooth, sweetish, easy-drinking dark mild

BEST BITTER

OG 1046°
Ingredients: pale malt (94%), wheat malt (3%), sugar and colour. Fuggles and Hallertau whole hops and hop oil

TASTING NOTES

Nose	Rich, tangy hop aroma with fruit notes developing
Palate	Full malt in the mouth with hop edge, long, delicate bitter-sweet finish
Comments	Cleansing, fine drinking quality bitter

INDEX

60/- Pale Ale, 24
6X, 210

70/- Special, 24

80/- Export, 24

ABC Bitter, 101
Adnams & Company, 122
Allied Breweries, 16
Alloa Brewery Company Ltd, 16
Ansells Best Bitter, 100
Ansells Mild, 100
Anvil Bitter, 262
Anvil Light, 262
Anvil Mild, 262
Anvil Strong Ale or XXXX, 263
Archers Ales Ltd, 186
Archibald Arrol's 70/, 16
Archibald Arrol's 80/, 16
Arkell Best Bitter (3Bs), 188
Arthur Guinness Son and Co, 163
ASB, 187
Ash Vine Bitter, 217
Ash Vine Brewery, 217

Badger Best Bitter, 201
Ballard's Brewery Ltd, 169
Bank's Mild Ale, 77
Banks & Taylor Brewery Ltd, 124
Banks's, 77
Banks's Bitter, 77
Barclay Perkins, 60
Barron Brewery, 218
Bass (Tadcaster), 43
Bass Brewing (Burton), 78
Bass Brewing (Wolverhampton), 80
Bass Mitchells & Butlers Ltd, 79
Baz's Bonce Blower, 110
BB, 193
BBB, 197
BBBB, 221
Beacon Bitter, 86
Bear Ale, 30

Beaumanor Bitter, 97
Beechwood Bitter, 152
Beer Engine, 219
Belhaven 60/, 17
Belhaven 70/, 17
Belhaven 80/, 18
Belhaven 90/, 18
Belhaven Brewery Company Ltd, 17
Benchmark, 190
Benfro Bitter, 247
Benfro Extra, 247
Benskins Best Bitter, 101
Berrow, 220
Best Cellar, 275
Best Mild, 155, 270, 274, 283
Best Mild Ale, 84
Big End Brewery, 44
Big Lamp Bitter, 32
Big Lamp Brewery, 32
Bitter (BB), 122
Bitter Ale, 224
Black Adder, 137
Black Country Bitter, 88, 92
Black Country Mild, 92
Black Country Special Bitter, 93
Black Knight Stout, 112
Blackawton Bitter, 222
Blackawton Brewery, 221
Boddingtons Bitter, 253
Boddingtons Breweries Ltd, 253
Boddingtons Mild, 253
Bombardier, 146
Border Bitter, 107
Border Mild, 106
Borve Ale, 19
Borve Brew House, 19
Borve Extra Strong Ale, 19
Bosun Best Bitter, 204
Bosun's Bitter, 235
Brew 69, 120
Brewery Bitter, 237
Brewhouse Ale, 142
Bridge Bitter, 82
Bridport Bitter (BB), 202
Broadside, 123
Broadsman Bitter, 147
Broughton Brewery Ltd, 20
Buckley's Best Bitter, 244
Buckley's 4X, 244

Buckley's Dark, 244
Buckley's Mild, 244
Bullion, 141
Bullmastiff, 242
Bunces Brewery, 190
Burglar Bill's, 46
Burt's Brewery Ltd, 192
Burton Best Bitter, 107
Burton Bridge Brewery, 82
Burton Mild, 86
Burtonwood Brewery PLC, 256
Butcombe Bitter, 223
Butcombe Brewery Ltd, 223
Butser Brew Bitter, 197

Caledonian 70/, 21
Caledonian 80/, 21
Caledonian Brewery Company Ltd, 21
Caledonian Porter, 21
Caledonian Strong Ale, 22
Captain Smith's Strong Ale, 116
Cask Bitter, 257
Cask Mild, 257
Castle Eden, 35
Castle Eden Ale, 35
Castletown Bitter, 280
Celebration Ale, 159
Centurion Best Bitter, 37
Charles Wells, 146
Charrington IPA, 80
Chester's Best Bitter, 74
Chester's Best Mild, 74
Chiltern Ale, 152
Chiltern Brewery, 152
Chiswick Bitter, 161
Christmas Ale, 116, 135
Clark, 45
Clark's HB, 45
Clark's Traditional, 45
College Ale, 159, 179
Cornish Brewery Co, 225
Cornish Original, 226
Cotleigh Brewery, 227
Country Best Bitter, 134
Courage Ltd, 224
Cropton Brewery, 47
Crouch Vale Brewery Ltd, 128
Crown 1041, 245

Crown Buckley, 244
Crown SBB, 245

D Batham & Son Ltd, 81
Daniel Thwaites PLC, 273
Dark Maidstone Ale, 171
Dark Mild, 126, 158, 256, 270
Dark Star, 164
Dark XXXX, 180
Darley Dark Mild, 70
Darley Thorne Best Bitter, 70
Dartmoor Best, 234
Dartmoor Strong, 234
Davenports Brewery Ltd, 84
Deakins Downfall, 95
Delph Strong Strong, 81
Devizes Bitter, 210
Devon Glory, 218
Directors Bitter, 225
Dolphin Bitter, 204
Donnington Brewery, 193
Dorchester Bitter, 195
Dorset Original IPA, 195
Double Chance Bitter, 52
Double Dagger, 268
Double Dragon, 246
Draught Bass, 78
Draught Steam Bitter, 226

Eagle Bitter, 146
EB, 130
Ebony Dark, 242
Eldridge Pope & Co PLC, 195
Elgood & Sons Ltd, 130
Emperor Ale, 38
English Guineas Stout, 50
Enoch's Hammer, 51
ESB, 266
ESB (Extra Special Bitter), 162
Essex Porter, 129
Everards Brewery Ltd, 86
Exevalley Bitter, 218
Exhibition Bitter, 237
Exmoor Ale, 229
Exmoor Ales Ltd, 229
Exmoor Dark, 229

Exmoor Gold, 230
Extra, 123

Farmer's Glory, 211
Farmers Ale, 233
Farmhouse Bitter, 248
Felinfoel Best Bitter, 246
Felinfoel Brewery Ltd, 246
Fellrunners, 259
Festival Ale, 83
Festive, 176
Flowers IPA, 212
Flowers Original, 213
Forbes Best Bitter, 131
Forbes Oulton Broad Brewery, 131
Forty Four, 222
Fortyniner, 205
Franklins, 48
Franklins Bitter, 48
Frederic Robinson & Co Ltd, 269
Fremlins Bitter, 170
Fremlins Ltd, 170
Friary Meux Best Bitter, 101
Fuller Smith & Turner PLC, 161

Garthwaite Special, 45
GB Mild, 264
George Bateman & Son Ltd, 126
George Gale & Co Ltd, 196
Gibbs Mew PLC, 199
Gladiator Bitter, 37
Glenny Brewery Co, 153
Goacher's, 171
Golden Mild, 64
Goose Eye Brewery, 69
Greenalls Ltd, 257
Greene King Abbot Ale, 133
Greene King IPA, 132
Greene King & Sons PLC, 132
Greenmantle Ale, 20
GSB, 130
Guernsey Brewery Co (1920) Ltd, 282
Guinness Extra, 163
Guv'nor's Special Brew, 232

Hadrian Brewery Ltd, 37

Hall & Woodhouse Ltd, 201
Halls Harvest Bitter, 102
Hammerhead, 46
Hancock's HB, 250
Hancock's PA, 250
Hanson's Bitter, 88
Hanson's Mild Ale, 88
Hansons Brewery, 88
Hardys & Hansons Ltd, 89
Harrier SPA, 227
Hartleys (Ulverston) Ltd, 258
Harvey & Son (Lewes) Ltd, 173
Harviestoun 80/, 23
Harviestoun Brewery Ltd, 23
Head Cracker, 148
Headbanger, 187
Headstrong, 222
Henry Wadworth IPA, 210
Hereford Bitter, 119
Hereford Supreme Bitter, 119
Heritage Bitter, 90
Heritage Brewery, 87
Heritage Brewery Co, 90
Hermitage Best Bitter, 183
Hicks Special, 236
Highgate Brewery Ltd, 91
Highgate Mild, 91
Higsons Ltd, 260
Hilden Ale, 277
Hilden Brewery, 277
Hobgoblin, 154
Hogshead, 207
Holdens Brewery Ltd, 92
Holt Plant & Deakin Ltd, 94
Holts Entire, 94
Home Bitter, 96
Home Brewery Ltd, 96
Home Mild, 96
Hook Norton Brewery Co Ltd, 155
Horndean Special Bitter, 198
Hoskins & Oldfield, 98
Hoskins Brewery PLC, 97
Hoxton Best Bitter, 165
HPA, 119

HSD, 236
Hydes' Anvil Brewery Ltd, 262

Imperial Russian Stout, 60
Ind Coope Best Bitter, 102
Ind Coope Burton Brewery Ltd, 100
Ind Coope Draught Burton Ale, 102
India Pale Ale, 78
IPA, 203, 239
Isle of Man Breweries Ltd, 279

J Arkell & Sons Ltd, 188
J W Cameron & Co Ltd, 34
J.C. & R.H. Palmer Ltd, 202
J.W. Lees & Co Ltd, 264
James Shipstone & Sons Ltd, 114
Janner's Ale, 230
Janner's Christmas Ale, 231
Janner's Old Dark, 231
Janner's Old Original, 231
JD Dry Hop Bitter, 225
Jennings Bros PLC, 263
John Arkell Bitter (BB), 188
John Smith's Tadcaster Brewery, 59
John Smiths Bitter, 59
John Smiths Magnet, 59
John Smiths Yorkshire Bitter, 59
Johnson's Bitter, 179
Joseph Holt & Co Ltd, 261
Joshua Tetley & Son Ltd, 66
JTS XXX, 103

Kimberley Best Bitter, 89
Kimberley Best Mild, 89
King & Barnes Ltd, 175
Kingfisher Ale, 227
Kingsdown Ale, 189
Knight Porter, 111
Knightly Bitter, 111

Landlord, 65
Larkins Brewery Ltd, 177
LBA Mild, 282
Leadboiler, 50
Light, 241
Light 5 Star, 43
Light Ale, 158
Light Maidstone Ale, 171
Linfit, 49
Linfit Bitter, 49
Linfit Mild, 49
Linfit Special, 49
Lloyds, 103
Local Bitter, 214
London Porter, 165
London Pride, 161
Lorimer's Best Scotch, 40
Lumley Old Ale, 184

M&B Brew XI, 79
M&B Mild, 79
Maclay & Company Ltd, 24
Maiden's Ruin, 112
Malton Brewery Co Ltd, 52
Malton Pale Ale, 52
Mansfield Brewery Ltd, 105
Marston Thompson & Evershed PLC, 106
Martin Ales, 179
Martin Brewery, 135
Master Brew Best Bitter, 182
Master Brew Bitter, 182
Matthew Brown Ltd, 255
Mauldons Bitter, 136
Mauldons Brewery, 136
Mauldons Porter, 136
McEwan 70/, 26
McEwan 80/, 26
McEwan and Younger, 26
McMullen & Sons Ltd, 134
Mercian Mild, 107
Merlin's Ale, 20
Merman XXX, 22
Mild Ale, 81, 114
Mild XXXX, 43
Mill Brewery, 230
Miners Arms Brewery, 232
Mitchells, 266

Mole's Brewery, 202
Mole's Cask Bitter, 202
Moonraker, 265
Moorhouses Brewery (Burnley) Ltd, 267
Morland & Co PLC, 157
Morrells Brewery Ltd, 158
Museum Ale, 61

Nethergate Bitter, 138
Nethergate Brewery Co Ltd, 138
Newcastle Breweries Ltd, 39
Nix Wincott Brewery, 139
Norfolk Porter, 147
North & East Riding Brewers Ltd, 54
Northern Clubs Federation Brewery Ltd, 36

Oak, 268
Oak Best Bitter, 268
Oakhill, 233
OB Bitter, 254
OB Mild, 253
Okells Bitter, 279
Okells Mild, 279
Old, 122
Old Ale, 175
Old Baily, 105
Old Bill, 87
Old Brewery Bitter, 61
Old Buzzard, 228
Old Devil, 215
Old Eli, 50
Old Fart, 57
Old Genie, 33
Old Growler, 138
Old Hookey, 156
Old Horizontal, 62
Old Jock, 20
Old Lubrication, 44
Old Maidstone Ale, 172
Old Manor, 23
Old Masters, 157
Old Merlin Mild, 111
Old Mill Brewery, 140
Old Nigel, 98
Old Nix, 139
Old Oak Ale, 268
Old Original, 87
Old Peculier, 69
Old Smokey, 191
Old Spot Prize Ale, 207
Old Thumper, 206
Old Timer, 211

Old Tom, 58, 271
Old Vic, 238
Old XXXX Ale, 57
Olde Grumble, 215
Ordinary, 166
Original, 144
Original AK, 134
Original Bitter, 249
Orkney Brewery, 28
Owd Bob, 53
Owd Rodger, 108
Own Ale, 232
OX (Old Expensive), 83

PA, 143, 150, 173
Pale Ale, 173
Parish Bitter, 109
Parish Brewery, 109
Pedigree Bitter, 108
Pembrokeshire's Own Ales Ltd, 247
Pendle Witches Brew, 267
Penn's Ale, 97
Phoenix XXX, 148
Pickwick's Porter, 53
Pig's Ear, 208
Pigor Mortis, 208
Pilgrim Brewery, 180
Piston Bitter, 44, 219
Pitfield Bitter, 164
Pitfield Brewery, 164
Plassey Brewery, 248
Plympton Best, 234
Plympton Brewery, 234
Poachers Ale, 109
Pompey Royal, 170
Poole Best Bitter, 204
Poole Brewery, 204
Porter, 25, 65, 83, 178
Premier Ales Ltd, 111
Premier Bitter, 267
Premium, 97, 275
Prince Bishop Ale, 32
Prize Old Ale, 198
Progress, 181

R.W. Randall Ltd, 283
Rail Ale, 219
Rapier Pale Ale, 141
Raven Ale, 28
Rayments BBA (Best Bitter Ale), 133
Real Draught Bitter, 282
Red Dragon Dark, 241
Reepham Brewery, 141
Riding Dark Mild, 108

Riding Traditional Bitter, 105
Ringwood Brewery, 205
Robinwood Brewers & Vintners, 56
Royal Oak, 195
Ruddles Best Bitter, 113
Ruddles Brewery Ltd, 113
Ruddles County, 113

S.A. Brain & Co Ltd, 241
S.H. Ward & Co Ltd, 70
SA Best Bitter, 241
Salisbury Best Bitter, 199
Sam Powell Brewery, 248
Samson Ale, 40, 249
Samuel Smith Old Brewery (Tadcaster), 61
Samuel Webster & Wilsons Ltd, 71
Sarah Hughes Brewery, 99
Sarah Hughes Mild, 99
SAS, 128
SBA, 194
Selby (Middlebrough) Brewery Ltd, 58
Select, 62
Sheffield Best Bitter, 70
Shefford Bitter, 124
Shefford Old Dark (SOD), 125
Shefford Old Strong (SOS), 125
Shefford Pale Ale (SPA), 125
Shepherd Neame, 181
Shipstone, 84
Skullcrusher, 104
Sleeper Heavy, 220
Smiles Brewing Co Ltd, 237
Smugglers Stout, 142
Son of a Bitch, 243
Sovereign Bitter, 177
SPA, 151
Special, 33
Special Ale, 36
Special Best Bitter, 245
Special Bitter, 43, 151, 166
Special Reserve, 277

Special Strong Bitter, 47
Springfield Bitter, 80
Squires Bitter, 136
St Austell Brewery Co Ltd, 235
Stanley Bitter, 135
Stocks Doncaster Brewery, 62
Stocks Best Bitter, 52
Stonehenge Best Bitter, 215
Stones Best Bitter, 63
Strong Country Bitter, 213
Strongarm, 34
Strongarm Premium, 35
Suffolk Punch, 137
Surrey Bitter, 180
Sussex Best Bitter (BB), 174
Sussex Bitter (PA or Pale Ale), 173
Sussex Bitter, 175
Sussex Brewery, 183
Sussex Mild, 175
Sussex Old (XXXX), 174
Sussex Pale Ale, 184

T & R Theakston Ltd, 68
T.D. Ridley & Sons Ltd, 143
Talisman, 181
Tally Ho, 124
Tally Ho!, 203
Tanglefoot, 201
Tawny Bitter, 227
Taylor Walker Best Bitter, 103
Tennent Caledonian Breweries Ltd, 29
Tennent's 80/, 29
Tetley Bitter, 66, 271
Tetley Dark Mild, 272
Tetley Imperial, 67
Tetley Mild, 66, 271
Tetley Walker Ltd, 271
The Bishop's Tipple, 200
Theakston Best Bitter, 39
Thomas Greenall's Original Bitter, 258
Thomas Hardy's Ale, 196
Thomas Sykes Old Ale, 90
Thompsons, 239
Tiger Bitter, 86

Timothy Taylor & Co Ltd, 64
Tinners Bitter, 236
Titanic Brewery, 115
Titanic Premium, 115
Tolly Cobbold, 144
Topsy Turvey, 221
Traditional Ale, 177
Traditional Bitter, 34, 84, 140
Traditional Mild, 140
Traquair House Ale, 30
Traquair House Brewery, 30
Trophy, 74
Trough Brewery Ltd, 69
Truman Best Bitter, 209
Two Henrys Bitter, 139
Two Pints Best Bitter, 47

Uley Bitter, 207
Uley Brewery Ltd, 207
Ushers Best Bitter, 209
Ushers Brewery Ltd, 209

Varsity, 159
Vaux Best Bitter, 40
Vaux Breweries Ltd, 40
Vaux Double Maxim, 41
Victory Ale, 127
Village Bitter, 186
VIP, 104
VPA (Ventnor Pale Ale), 192

W.H. Brakspear & Sons PLC, 150
Wadworth & Co Ltd, 209
Walker Best Bitter, 273

Walker Bitter, 272
Walker Mild, 272
Walker Winter Warmer, 273
Warrior Ale, 184
Wassail, 169
Websters Choice, 73
Websters Green Label, 72
Websters Yorkshire Bitter, 72
Welsh Brewers Ltd, 250
Wem Best Bitter, 85
Wem Special Bitter, 85
Wessex Bitter, 226
West Country Pale Ale, 212
Wethered SPA, 213
Wethereds Bitter, 212
Wethereds Winter Royal, 213
Wherry Best Bitter, 147
Whitbread (Cheltenham), 212
Whitbread (Sheffield), 74
Wild Boar, 69
William Clark's 68, 55
William Clark's EXB, 55
William Clark's Thistle Bitter, 54
William Clark's Thistle Mild, 54
William Stones, 63
Willie Warmer, 129
Wilsons Original Bitter, 72
Wilsons Original Mild, 71
Wiltshire Brewery Company PLC, 214
Wiltshire Traditional Bitter, 199
Winter Warmer, 46, 167

Witney Bitter, 153
Wobbly Bob, 269
Wood Brewery Ltd, 117
Wood's Christmas Cracker, 118
Wood's Parish Bitter, 117
Wood's Special Bitter, 117
Wood's Wonderful, 118
Woodforde's Norfolk Ales, 147
Woodham Bitter, 128
Worthington BB, 251
Worthington Dark, 251
Worthington M, 250
Worthington PA, 250
Worthington White Shield, 78
Wychwood Best, 153
Wye Valley Brewery, 119
Wyndham Bitter, 183

XB, 56, 68, 259
XB Bitter, 126
XL Bitter, 82
XL Old Ale, 93
Xmas Ale, 51
XX, 173
XX Mild, 132
XXX, 81, 143, 150, 193
XXXB Bitter, 127
XXXD Mild, 197
XXXL Mild, 197
XXXX, 145, 198, 235, 263
XXXX Porter, 205

Yates, 275
Yeoman Ale, 233
Young & Co PLC, 166
Younger Bitter, 26
Younger IPA, 26
Younger No 3, 27
Younger Scotch, 26